A CALL

Ralph

as I address you
a bee inspects the flowers of the window & the tapestry.

*

Your last hand
4 Diamonds
stands.

After 70 summers
Lara said *Already?*
when I told her
on Fathers Day
you had just died
in her 6th June.
I sent her on to the beach
with the rest of the century
while I wiped a little blood off the elevator button
& took the stairs up to your place in the west
one last move.
Living room
that's what you gave us.

Don't tell your mother you'd say to me
slipping me 5
or cranking the car older than me up to 30
on the postwar 40s Fraser Canyon highway
coming back from a call.

Up the coast
dressed as proud as a cedar tree
sharing a joint with me

talking about old roads.
You knew every town in Canada
& every state of America.

You raised a few welts on me
& I've taken a swipe at you.
I eat everything on my plate now.
You & Betty & Linda & I
we never bothered to split up.
I think we lived by pure memory.

You saw with your voice.
You talked.
I built my thought at home in that light.
You only ever owned what you'd say to see.

You had a great sneeze
& a death-defying laugh.

You knew
what I'm doing.

Betty told me that you & she made love
with your last afternoon together.
When she heard me say it in this poem
she blushed
& thought of you
& said *Yes*.

You taught me to lead with my life.

*

The bee danced its own way out.

REDOUBT

the dream ascared me

as you were all leaving me standing on the porch I asked for a mantra

the hated one turned, turning out to have the face of the loved one

of course, it goes, it goes

goodbye you guys

I'll see you again – who have you seen in me? – remember the other dream, the audience gathered, facing the sky ahead, where the hologram appeared for as long as it took to see, but not long enough to remember, & we applauded & you bowed to us – it was the image of the *father* – a word we'd only heard

how I feel & what I think about it all is not as significant to this poem as the fact you were all saying goodbye & leaving – I went & got velvet pants (they turned out to be velvet) for those who'd let themselves get wet – I was dismayed how small the pants were, you're still growing & it's me who's going (meaning, you're still going & it's me who's growing –?)

you're leaving me alone in the house with its living horror for me – a ton of hot dark shit pulled itself out of me spreading like a beaver's tail – that was upstairs while I was getting the pants – I rushed down the stairs (how does it start? – o what an awakening ...) & passed the bowing entreating dog at the entrance to the living room, the glass-panelled doors ajar (entranced?) – the dog is me, in that I bow to you with my pleading not to be left alone

alone with the evil movie zipping beelines through the house – but come to think of it, maybe they weren't aimed at me? – but at the time it seemed timeless & I wanted everyone to stay – I'd certainly try to deal with it if you didn't, but that's not for a moment yet – & the moment's gone o what an awakening! – you left me with what I know – it woke me up as I was re-entering the house to face the witching with my healthy terror – in the midst of which I found myself there, entering myself, intact

I was in my house
I was sleeping in my body
I woke from my body
goodbye – goodbye – I'm glad you can go

gatay gatay – para gatay – parasam gatay – bodhi svaha!

*

mine
the legacy the
other tradition

the pencil
father had held in his
business

CHAPTERS

WHEN IN LONDON

Sea*snails*withAnthonyforlunch=ENGLISHMONTREAL=ITALIAN
TORONTO=FRENCHMANITOBA=NATIVEINDIANREGINA=
UKRAINIANEDMONTON=EASTINDIANCENTRALBC=CHINESE
VANCOUVER=(thisisastorybaseonanunsentletter/whenIthoughtI
wascominghome)=Ihaven'tseenthiscommercialbefore=I'mnotgonna
listen=Yester*day*IwenttoPorto*bello*abcdeftofindtiny*gifts*foryou&you=
(itwasn'tthoselittlecrystal-cutearts/itwasaknotofCelticdesigninour
life)=hearingtheLiszt,notspellingit=ThenItookthetraintoHerneghij&

leapedlunchdiscussingwindow*frames*withEric,overwhiskey&beerin
thepubbythecleaner's=playingthegame,notlookingatit=(Icleanthistext
everytimeItypitout/it'sallaboutwhathappenedtomethereafterIcame
backhere)=I'mnotnecessarilyrigorousabouthowItransfarmthispiece
fromaworkintoaplay,butyou'llhearthepatterns=Italkedmyselfinto
place=thisisonethingIneverneedtoproof=(hereisadrawingofawindow
withaboo=holdingitopen=youcansaybooktoagoose'tilyou'rehooked
intolace=butGod'snoseiswhatthegoosewears)

CCMCfreejazzon=RailthroughtoO*xford*klmnop,buttheBaker*loo*qrst
wasshutdownbytheworkersrefusingtoride50,000wild*Scots*tothe
foot*ball*gameatWembly=OUTONESCAPE=(Ihearthatbynow,two
yearslate,thegraffitiintheUndergroundisinArabic/andthatinB.C.,
herointrafficing,at$255million,isthefifthlargestindustry,evenlarger
thanfishing's1976$165million)=nationallydopeisan$8.6billionbusiness
by'82,notcountingbooze&tobacco=SoIwalkedtotheBaker*St.*uvwxyz,
short*cutting*throughSel*fridge's*departmentstoretocheckoutthe
mensunder*wear*bcdefghijkwhereIonceworked=WESTINDIAN
LONDON=(IrememberthestaffloungeatHarrod's,too,whereoldold
meninblackblacksuitssat&sippedthought&scaredmewiththeirhole
lifetimesthere/thelongestmovieIeversawisstillmovingattheLascaux
Cave=painshinesthroughyou,evenwhenitdoesn'thurt=Mywaytosee
thelovely*movie*aboutDavid,theCalifornia*painter*=absomaizalootly=(on
mymy,ABiggerSplash,hesaidthatifhe'dknownwhatthefilmacrewasup
to,hewouldn'thaveallowedit,butit'ssucagoodmovieofcoursehe'lletit
stand,&inthemovieyoucanseepeopleheportraysthinkingthesamething
abouthispaintingsofthem/lastweekadrugcompanypatentedanewlife-
form)=InevergottocallmymaternalgrandfatherHerm,butIremember
him,&hewasborninNovaScotiaaboutaquartercenturyafterMoby-Dick
waspublished,&hewasnamedafterMelvillebyhismother,hebeingher
thirdchilditwasherturntoname,&itwastheonlyChristiannamehegot,&
thebookI'mreadingwhiletypingoutthisfouryearsofwritingisMoby-
Dick,soofcoursetomyselfIrefertomymanuscriptasMoby-Jane=theeasy
*busride*toCamden*High*lmnopqfordinnerwithCharlotte,remembering
theGreek*cafe*inLondon*Ontario*,&whathockeycandotoalanguage=sorry
forthewayIcameontoyouthatday,C=(there'sareportinyesterday'saper
abouttwingirlswhodidn'tlearntospeaktheirparents'English&German
languages,butmadeuptheirown=Dugon,hausyoudinikin,duah,snup-
aduhah-weedie-dipanadihabana/IpublishedpoetryfortenyearsbeforeI
appliedtotheCanadaCouncilforanything)=he:Ialwaysthoughtthere
werelittlepeopleintheradio=she:&thentherewastv&youcouldseethem

Charlottelookssotiny=(sorilliant/5%ofCanadianartistsmakealiving
fromtheirwork)=Thai?Yeah,hewegomatch-boxinggrassagain=Sheis
verythin=(howtomakebeginningseparate/forevery$100spentonart
administration,2centsgoestoanartist)=linger/languor=finger/fanguor
=Intoinnocence=everydaymybabyringgottighteruntillgotitcutoff&
nowit'slostandthemarkitmadehasgrownawaybutI'mstilllefthanded=
(Canadalookedfarawayandraunch/arts,letters&sciencefor2.3%ofCBC
programming)=Sheisworking*hard*=IwasgonnagetahaircutbutIthink
I'lljustgetitrepaired=(it'snotwhattheitalicsmean,it'swhattheyotothe
meaning/theruleinourfridgeisdon'teatthelastofanyoneelse'sfood)=the
lasttimeIsawJudyGarlanditwasatthePNEafterashow,shewastryingto
getpastafanwhohadexactlythesamefaceashersbutotherwiseweighed
about300pounds=every*body*hereinLondonseemstoberunningalittle
scared=everybodyhereinVancouverstandsstillonescalators=(my
personallyricvoiceisonstrikeforbetteringingconditions/theartgallery's
latestmovewastoinstructtheguardsnottotalktothevisitors)=youmight
havereadOnlyinLondonbeforeinWhenPaperToday=Wespentthe
eveningwithAlan&Julia&Roslyn,onPrince*ofWales*rstuvwxy=I'm
almostbacktothebeginningofthebook=(thepotholesareherewords
droppedout/thebumpsarewherelettersremainunsent)=thebasisofthis
storyhearkensbacktoearlier,crazieryears,buttheyearsofthisbook,1978,
1979,1980,1981,1982,havebeeneminentlysensibleonmypart,asyou'llsee=
WetalkedabouttheMiddlezabc=mayIrecommendthatChapter31be
readaloudbyawhitewino=(thealphabetisjusttemporaryill/between
May1975&October1977)=onGranvilleMallfora$yougettogiveakida$=I
showedthemmyFardefghij*slides*,&playedthetapes&saidthepoems=if
you'vealwaysgotthebrakesonwhathappenswhenyoureallyhavetostop
it=(the12foothighmapofAfricaontheallaboveus,thelastwallleft
standingwhenthebuildingwassmasheddown/isalmostacontinent
smallerthanAfrica=priortothisfinalrevisionofWheninVancouver,I
glancedthroughthestory&hatedit,itwassuchutterbullshititwas
unutterable,likewhocares=watchoutforwriterswhocan*is*themselves
acrossthepage,butanyonetryingtofollowthemgetscreamedbyasudden
busloadofsleepingdrivers=youdon'thavetostartatthebeginning=At
mid*night*Iturnedintothelast*trainhome*=thetroublewiththearmedforces
istheydon'thavepeoplelikeyouinthem=(wegrew/whenwestopped
leavingpartsofourselvesbehind)=I'malittlerashundermymoustache&
you'realittlezitunderyourtit&here'stolookingwithoureyesfullfrom
hereonin

renewyourquandry,doyourlaundry=Thenightbeforethat,Friday
night,wasGlascow*night*attheSound*Poetry*klmnopqr=thatwasclose,the

thought,itstartedthinking,expectingmetocomealongforthewalktothe
nextcigarette=(thewindowisawideropeningthanashingit/Glascowis
onthevergeofanewlanguage,andit'ssodistantfromEnglishthattheBBC
hastotranslateitforbroadcast)=theumbrella'snotforsmoking=Igave
Nicholson*amickeyofBCliquor*board*OneCrown*stuvwx&acassette*tape*to
drinkitinto=line&winter=word&year=syllable&decade=letter&
century=(Ileftmyselfunlocked&itwastoolatetoreturn&itleanedmeout/
BingCrosbywasthelastbigmiddleclasshero)=Eaton'sless&enjoyingit
more=mistake&seafood=GrancevilleneedsLitter=drinkingatLeo's
withthebabymoney=That*afternoon*I'dseentheShaker*exhibition*atthe
Victoria&Albertyzabcd=oIgetit,squeezethesphincter&therootofthe
cockmuscles&letthatcentreofsensationbetweenasshole&ballsradiate
freeelectricity=(whenyoucallmedear,itfillsmyelfpitswithheart,aching/
nothinghappenswhenyoudon'tcall)=whenyoucallmecheap,itfillsmy
ogreprotuberanceswithliver,thrilling/everythinggoesstillwhenyoudo
call=LookuptheShakers=(lookutotheShakers/theywereeasyworkers)

people&redants=soldierspecieswhofightthemselvestothedeath=
This*afternoon*IpacedouttheVowel*Test*inthegreen*avenues*ofKensington
efghijk=thedistantdifferencesthroughwhichyoucanhearvowelsgrowl=
(thiswaslongbeforethealarmatwasevenborn/andbeforeIre-titledthe
poemLungDistance)=theHailPoetrychorusinW.S.Gilbert'sPiratesof
Penzance=Itwasasilent*soundpoem*IperformedjustoutofsightofThe
*Video*Imnoatthe*Serpentine*pqrstuv=don'tdespair,ifthere'sanyhopeit's
inus&inthechildren,herdingthemchromosomeshome=(hemediumisa
mess,butthatwasbeforethepuncontrolpill/sherarelyisamiss,butthat
wasaftertheact)=thetimethecarriagestuck&Ihadtowritelinesofone
l
e
t
t
e
r
=Icame*home*tonighttotheLiver*pool*vwxy,&laydownforanhourto
unbendintimetothelast*fourhours*ofthehousehold'sSunday13*hour*lunch=
tothetuneofWeltHickey'simmortalBalladoftheBeggarwiththelittle
SignonhisCupsayingAlmostBlind=(awiseinconsistencyistheallyof
roadminds/poetryisnotanact)=whenIwasakidinRupertthetimeIwas
watchingthebigguysflyingtheirkitesonmiles&milesofstringwayout
overthepigfarm&thearmybase,thisbeingearly'40s,&thesoldiers
shootingthekitesdownforsport=thescareinthegrownup'svoiceaswe
watchedtheHurricanesfromtheTerracebasedogfightingintheafternoon

sky=But it was an *other* Sun*day* entirely, the one with the serious *case* of wine
bought 3 *weeks ago* before the price went up, meant to last all *summer*,
suddenly all *gone*=I think so you drink so=(laughing at Me babbling on tv/
an open brook)=when everything went wrong I thought it was me & you
thought it was you, what a nice couple we turned out to be=No sooner
than....=your face or mine?=(if you weren't there, you can be no/if you were
there, you helped write the book)=I thought the beach would break in two
when I said, carelessly, 'Do you come here often?' but you do

read the title, say the poem=the vertically integrated poet=Bunting,
looking 3 *months younger* than the 20th zabcdef, stands at the National *Poetry*
ghi, drinking, beside the bronze of Basil=the word replaced by ghi is "bar",
Basil standing there beside a bust of himself, ignoring some ignorant
comment of mine about Wordsworth=(jklmnopqrstuvwxy/Zed is a
man's first name in Missouri)=actually, he ignored my comment while he
was sitting, & he moved to the bar to get away from what I might say next

THE NEW ERA MARATHON

1 *they didn't wait for my cue*

    the rest of the way
    the crest of the wave

2 *changing lanes*

    we've had nothing but sunshine
    these last couple of those
    paradoxes Vancouver is unknown from

3 *down the high*

    15 clicks
    way out to the sticks

4 *how are we doing for what more can a man ask*

    they don't make
    sitting in the comfort of your own houses of parliament
    sauce bottle
    like they used to do
    they

5 *he runs that film through the camera*

    a kilometer being smaller than a mile
    makes it easier to stare in belief
    through the distance you live in

6 *of essence of*

    essence of essence

7 *on in from here*

    the way we haven't been changing
    the beginning of Canada
    fast enough

8 *he might not make it*

    he'll make it

9 *running at the mouth*

    to be
    get
    here
    there

10 *the surface of reality*

think about those toes
sweating especially for this occasion

11 *the light of speed*

the speed of light
plus
the speed at which you're thinking
equals
speech

12 *making a living*

the situation
includes you
hanging on

13 *right left*

this is not gas for less
this was made right here in the palm of my hand
out at the next step after that
this

14 *don't move, Taki*

a man wants
not to miss
an inch

15 *sculpture*

a feet
performing

COASTING

dis (1st coffee) banding the smoky sunfilled dream
colours in my face

the 2nd cup for a clear memory
I dreamed that BC joined Mexico

you dreamt that everyone had bare feet
& all the shoes tossed in to put on were yours

the birds are words
bubbling over with music

the mosquitos are working out a zone offensive
practicing on astral bodies

morning
the past is dew

Wednesday

Edam is made backwards
Cheezus
it's not raining & it's not Christmas
my turn backing out of Canada now

the U.S.A. is bigger than B.C.
& smaller than A.D.
49th Parallel Pissing Permitted On
& on how to use this poem

papier
surfin
the Sea of Seattle
aspiring dissolving in 100% rain this afternoon

19 20 21
Vancouver Seattle San Francisco
August 20 1978
2 greeds before yesterdegree

no feet without people
no peanut without garlic
no coffee without sleep
no girl without within

Thursday

a couple little koffs on the page
& that's it for out loud
leave Seattle listening to the sky escape
no-one but me on the 2 worst seats in the bus

paper plum bag squash
veracity here I come
America is the easy answer
I'm the still question mark

I slept curled up on that one
please lock door
to turn on
or a going going gone

I wasn't looking for goodness
gracious me
but thank you
any old way

I never met an arbutus tree I didn't like
I don't like like
like like likes like
I do like the likes of me

Friday

hi
I spent the day trying to hear something to say fast
after driving past Grenada/Gazelle south of Yreka
I see

from the big black lady in the royal blue muu-muu on Market street
bend down to the poor drunk man & kiss him
to the telephone pole that snapped itself off at the root
& fell down across the car parked there by the Seattle Farmers Market

the front man at the U.S. border looking at me in the back of the van
& saying, 'One of the kids?'
the newborn breasts
of my #6 daughter

the sound of David kicking through Jeanne's door
'Why did you do it?'
'I was angry.'
'I don't know what you were angry about.'

hey – all you creative people out there
you are listening to the Canadian language
always open & then some
it left right now saying, 'The future is a copy.'

Saturday

Night in Tunisia
4
someone's missing
those were shots

you took them
we tried not to believe it
but we could tell someone was there
we could tell the truth

it's comin' it's comin'
our legs are too long
give our names
take our names

keep your life
come with us
I'm gonna be here
I'm gonna be there

I'm never anywhere am I
there's lots of room
we made it
you'll make it

Sunday

the lamp light spins in the wind-o glass at night
so does the sun at dawn, into my sleep
if I can get there in time
to the moon crossing the sun deck

I don't do any building
I do the dishes, sweep the floor, take the pictures
share the reading & writing

I bet it's steamy in Berkeley

it's cool here, its own
hot inland pulls the weathers over San Francisco Bay all day
the air's fast all right
but it'll take longer to say September

events fly at me
like: everyone's on wheels or tossing balls or bumming smokes
having a machined good time in the park this aft
& I'm eventually rolling around town too, catching all the lites

silently learning what went wrong
engaging the moment within the gesture
seeing without being a scene
reading every poem

Monday

there's no time tonight
we don't need to remember going to sleep
you were as young in the dream as a dream
where we lose the time

the children won't settle down
to anything but laughs or sobs
or hiccups or else
where we find the time

BzzART's smooth & soft but the doors didn't open
that took 20 minutes
this takes 20 lines
I've been here in '48 '57 '69 & '78 for a good 20 days

while I'm here I'll love you with all my might
but no maybes
people are always giving me heart
& I'm always leaving it somewhere

let's call it a city
lost beginnings & loose ends
a bathtub for every spider
the morning haze clears 20,000 years

Tuesday

dog howling at the siren
wasp died on the arborite
o dear
I do like it here

I don't go into storms
where I have to leave my brag at the door
take a page
make a chain

your voices here come from the light here
it takes the dark
to tell where else you've grown up
fog prondl dada

you soon find out who
is the woman you're wrestling with
you always have to read your money
you don't have to read this

David socked out a warm tough fast-drying poem tonight
I missed a free earthquake yesterday
you can read the Chronicle over your morning vitamin
captives of the defined

there there

it's taken a week
& a half to run out of tobacco
& to water my wine
& to see you again

everyone hissed at the cats
when I suggested staying
there being the empty bed
& my empty head

sitting on the hot side of the ride
in the wind at the back
drying my hair & my shirt
& feeding my map

I want to keep the edge on our looks
so we can keep on talking

we we

working on roads
the structure of our life
making sense

body feels good
looking on
following meaning

gestures we can't re-use
no posing
no return

but we hardly know each other
dot that t
cross that i

your ease
my care

come come

we kissed & missed
she got the top of my head
I made off with her right nipple

like the driver said
'I gotta make a Right Here!' (in fact
he didn't & I'm going right on too)

I know I shouldn't have rained yesterday
I'm a clone from a batch of only 200
we are all liquids here

any moment now I'm gonna meet someone
I hope it's you
you know your own ground

half & half
a glass of golden tequila
a ride on Moby-Dick

going going

'reggae is not punk disco – wash those grease-stains in!
'disco comes out swinging – walk away!'

1st stop is for provisions at the Food co-op, on the Greyrabbit
    hop from San Francisco Bay to the Columbia River. I rode
    this same very light green old FLXIBLE bus when it was a
    hound to the Bay in 1948 from Burrard Inlet – big black dude
    beside me blowing my Kitsilano Kid mind full of wordsmoke –

'Bop City
'let's you & me
'Get Off Together
'I'll take ya t'
'BOP CITY!'

it still is
like a hand on the need

to fight or switch

suck rock
blow jazz

hear hear

oil farm
electric ranch

these hills
that grow

this gold
en grass

steel river
smooth enough to sing on

music
spoken here

it's all they forgot
to lose

tis
dance

SO SO

we stopped for a quick coffee & a slow piss at the Truckadero
& to let off the fly & let on a mosquito
& I'm the kind of passenger who notices
the kind of driver who looks over his shoulder to talk to us
riders of the evening star
I woke when the music stopped for a quick glance & a slow moment
I can think of a poem but I can't think of a poet
I don't know what you make of this but this is what I made of that
identify with the bus if you want to be spaced out
there's plenty of fear for every one of us to drive into
ink is the blood of history
the poem goes where it's needed
I keep pushing it away
not me! not me!

now now

22 hours to Portland
6 of them late
5 minutes to spare

I think us passengers were all last-minute replacements
we wore out but we didn't break down
it's still raining in Wash.

lots of talk showed through
but we had little to say
the trees are looking up

now it's a week later & this is written
I'm totally unwound
a picture for the blind

WRITE

THURSDAY

*

here goes

It sure feels good to leave town, pack the night before & tear up all undone writing. Let's see what I remember of it –

> *getting nowhere practice*

> turn the heat down
> & put a coat on
> & sit around for a few days

& then there was the cartoon of the framed buck on the wall with the title, The Last Dollar I Ever Made. I was gonna be a cartoonist once.

I forgot to pack some safes. The trouble with thinking up things ahead of time is it leaves you dead when you get there – like Vancouver, maybe not today, but yesterday. I voted for Gloria. Final results show that most people need to celebrate death for another couple of years yet.

This is a year & a week since last year's trip to Comox, so we'll call it a week ago. As I wrote then –

first ferry

the alarm clock only had to go off once
before I caught on to its trick

I can be like that
sleep all day

I can be like that
other meaning

the boys are are 8 & 10
mom is a cool 9

she sneezes 3 times
it out-crochets a light cpr blue sweater

dad's body sails to nanaimo
dad's soul long ago reached its goal

it's sitting up there on a lifeboat chewing the view
slowly increasing in value & tarnishing

Once there was a July dawn I slipped past those mountains as if they
were a woman sleeping. Today –

north vanish

cloud
beheads
mountain

I cropped three-quarters of the sweatband out of my French workers'
cap & it fits me again. Success goes to my head & comes out swell, low,
after the gale yesterday.

keep home growing

I bought a couple promises on the way to the ferry to the day
there's Stanley parked over there
Vancouver by green grass

I made my sister's bed today
to say nothing of my own is to say something
a wise investment

I take pictures you know
I gotta do something that costs
& is worth it

Point Grey isn't getting anywhere
(to the tune of
West Point Grey is Falling Down, Falling Down, Falling, falling

I don't need you afternoons
I need you
nights

this
costs
me

can poetry go the distance
against all those simultaneous multiple personalities?
can I eat for $2 CDN?

you have to hand it to the CPR
but don't let go of your ha ha
hand

   While you're reading this, I was reading The Sheltering Sky by Paul
Bowles, which I borrowed from Jerry On Hornby Island last week while
his house burned down. I was visiting Sheila. I said, 'Tell me everything
you know about this island. Start anywhere. Be as incomplete as you
like.'

'I know that Phil keeps his honey in a bucket.'

'Is the heron still there?'

'Yeah.'

'Is this something the heron is seeing? I mean, is everything something the heron is seeing?'

'Well, he's *not* seeing Phil's honey bucket.'

'But we are, & we're seeing the heron.'

'Yeah, but it's not ...'

'Doesn't it work that way?'

'No.'

'Oh. I thought it did. Who's that?'

'That's Rick. He lives at the other end of the bay.'

'Oh yeah, I can see the house from here – I'm not sure which one it is, but I can see it. I see them all.'

Check out the bar on my way to the deck, where I leave a wet ash on the white rail & meet a seagull & roll the roach into a cigarette without it going out, the red flag digging into the white sky for a place to file itself, flie –

you're the gull

the wake vanishes
the smoke doesn't

stretch & leap
the wind flys

it's you are hungry
not me

the dream of Vancouver Island

I'm rhyming with the ferry about now
arriving in Nanaimo in a moment just like this

the city fits the season
in starts & finishes

from the car-deck, open-stern, water-level, a spit from the wake
lean over & look up

if your hat fits
the Coast

cut the motors
slow down faster & faster

the motor cuts in & the wake picks up again a little
in that moment before entering the harbour

something falls asleep
& begins to dream

Nanaimo – it could be Dublin
the Key (to) Glory, Tokyo, delivering oranges at 40% more this year

Japan might solve a lot of Eire's troubles
by taking her under his wing

Ireland with Japanese Yen & Vancouver Island with British Sterling
are locked in a plate-tectonic battle-island war-race

them massive islands pursuing each other over the big drink
in fact of course at least as usual totally drunk

so ever so slowly, it's such a balmy movie, the islands collide
& everyone decides the South Pacific is there to stay that way

they sink their foreign capitals & surrender to Bali, the better to be
Vancouver Ireland!

(last week it pissed rain
& I found the bus depot a lot faster)

By bus to Courtenay. The heating systems all just caught up (ready for
tomorrow) to the day before yesterday here in the Southwest Territo-
ries. The tickets have cost me $8.80 CDN out of my last $20 CDN of credit &
that leaves CDN 10 cents for a call to Brad & then there's the penny I saved
by not having a lid on my coffee to go down Robson Street this morning
which with the change from Linda's coats' pockets & the dozen dusty
empties was just enough as you'll see. Flash past Pacemaker Auto-
motive. That's what I mean by *outer doubt*. The shell the food lives in.
Delicious people in all the shiny cars. This bus is a feast fit for the time it
takes. This is long before I get my teeth really fixed. I didn't get a grant. I
know too much. I write well into the sense of healthy, as healthy as a tree
on a DND Site can be. The girl in front, who also had to wait forever for
news of a grant, was surprised to see the guy sitting next to her ('Were
you on the ferry too?' 'Not that one.') & they each left on the spurs of the
moments today it turns out & she is telling him the story of a man in the
iron mask. Outer doubt. Leading to inner din. Let's up & get somewhere
they never named & I sure won't & don't you dare say anything about
this except this or it will just melt in your mouth. I come as I am & that's
the way I want to stay. When I saw the El Morocco I knew I was in the
right valley.

I phoned Brad but he arrived himself, leaving me stuck with a Cana-
dian dime, so I bought a tiny space-shuttle to orbit to the kid; & the
penny, one like untold tonnes of Canadian pennies, was the tax on my
all-expense-paid holiday in Comox, the prize I won a night later at

Scrabble in overtime, costing Brad his Friday night at the Lorne spent at home instead. The Lorne is just about the oldest pub in BC. Brad drinks with the Pope & the grandson of the man who invented the staple & the grand-daughter of the man who invented the vacuum tube & the true descendant of the man arrested on the road 40 miles from Ottawa on the mistaken belief that he'd murdered D'Arcy McGee, April 7 1886, 68 years before I was born, to the day. This is the local. On Thursday I drank it & on Saturday I eschewed it. The Pope's colours are red & blue & white. He has a Habs ring. I kissed it. If he's the Pope, I'm Canada's Top Poet.

FRIDAY

*

hung o'er

I don't wear glasses
to whet my attention I sit in the smoke
& polish my black AUDITOR'S FINE PT. 400F 59 RB LINDY USA pen
(which I threw away
next Valentine's day)
while the seal balances the ball
& ink runs out of the family &
there's Brad at the window
running the lipscape off the landstick
we couldn't get the oil to run into the stove
it's all lies by the Time Life negazine runs it
the sky's got the runs
all my stockings get is long walks
the jellyfish run in suicide schools
the ashtrays run all night
Irun/run2/towards/wordsto/together

(Yeah, well I'm back home typing this all out the following Tuesday, still reading The Sheltering Sky, still haven't had a bath. Keeps me safe. The tv is on, full of soundless fury. Fan is short for fanatic. Fanatic is short for fantastic. 'I saw a *fantastic*' massacre on tv last night – they did it to *themselves*!' 'Did you survive it?' See that little flash in the upper right-hand corner of the screen? That's a slug. We have 30 seconds. The mike's in the picture. We're not in love. The mike's on the milk. 'Let's go find someone we like,' said the wife to the mistress. Closing bracket.

SATURDAY

*

white

ever
green
except
today

forever after

the big kid
is called that

for a while

alone
read
eat
write
drink
get warm
go out & piss
curse my stupidity
smoke
get warm

quit for the sake of freedom
make a list
listen

well made

that's a light bulb
I hope he made it to Hud & Helen's all right
he said he'd walk back
there he is driving up
he made it past Pritchard

SUNDAY

*

keeping motion in things

I want to give some back but would you like a camel?
whoozat but that's Dixie's sister but everybody's some 1 else here
the news but it happened while we were talking about it
watch closely but there is a cat but doing just that

Brad & I had some strong words last night – the argument – we didn't
record it again this year – we got as far as Casablanca before we agreed
that we don't get made like we used to – it's been perfectly safe for me
here – it was cold enough & I was warm enough – most of the stories he
told me were about people here making peace with each other – years
are very important here – we laughed about the difference between a
picture of us alone & a picture of us in company – we unlocked the con-
clusion we reached & entered the Magic Theatre again – on the screen the
woman (who was played by the future) was leaving with the man

(who was played by the past) while the bogey, the viewer (who was played by the present) was giving them a point of departure – they'll be back – we felt fearless fair & free – we worked on the winter schedule – when he'll stop reading & start writing & I'll stop writing & start reading – we are working on the world – the one we shelter from the sky

beauty

What do you take for beauty?
Do you want to get it or get rid of it?
I want it to live like me.
I take my time.
What if I give my time?
Then it won't be yours anymore.
I don't have to give much do I?

The stove hums.
The teapots dance on it.
The fridge gurgles at the food.
Silence.

You don't have much to give.
Beauty is always such a rush.
Beauty is never much of a hurry.
But I can see how it will end.
If it bothers you don't peek.
But I can't go on blindly like this.
She must be very beautiful.
She knows.
That's impossible.
I told her.

The cat purring on my shoulder.

workshop

that little
yon green slug spotted with black
has just gotten back on horizontal
after a trip down the salmonberry stalk from where I wrapped him
after interrupting his chewing at some papers rotting on the floor
where he'd been making a nuisance of himself this week
bothering the cats & tieing up the toilet
so it's back on the road for you my fake little rodent
keep cool of heart
& don't go trying to be so smart

that
that carbide steel chip
that shot off
that sawblade needed to be
that sharp to miss us by
that little

    & you tell me what I was doing

        what you did was 6 beer before dinner & wine
        4 or 5 brandies w/coffee after
        not to mention the eventuality
        of the other bottle of wine
        & the other world of dope
        until a few last beer

        call the radio
        turn down
        Jonestown
        kill the radio

        T
        I
        L
        T

Monday

*

what's around the corner – the forties?

Willy Messerschmidt is dead but Mickey Mouse dies on
when I write with ink I don't lose my mistakes
what this country needs is a good 5-year investigative poem
a mistake is when just shutting up would have avoided all that
in the meantime, the Troller/Net-fisherman's War surfaces
      at the fault of the situation (Port Hardy) (wall to wall fighting)
      but nobody's asking the fish
journalism follows the story by the smell & everyone eats it up
poetry leads the story by the nose & no-one swallows it
there's where the cat bit through 4 pages in the middle of the Bowles –
I like to carry a bowl with me – I have an old Japanese porcelain teacup
      occupied by me rolled in a sweater in a bag in a bus to Nanaimo
what happens to money with capitalism is what happens to cells
      with cancer
a new owner fixes any old car
they were celebrating life up in Comox
people see more of each other than the city
& the more you see the more you free
YOU DESERVE A SPACE TODAY
AT THE MEMORIAL ARENA
SEE THE OTHER SIDE
goin' down the Coast again
are
beaut
us
look at all those trees in the sunshine today
it's a wonder we don't have better newspapers
here comes a guy in a Canadiens toque & sweater & an houndstooth
      scarf
& a car with snow frozen blue on it in reverse offering you a light in the
      wind
let him sign you up for a course at the Comox Valley School
      of Fried Prawns

the 4 o'clock ferry back downtown

the day is yea-bright
the night is yea-long

that cloud over there in the late west has the substance of mountains
that smoke from the mill *is* the substance of mountains

when I saw today out here
I wished for you
jeune fille

against the twilight
the birds show me their substance
the black of their silhouettes
against the flight

a man comes & lowers the flag out of the night
I walk the other way

I sit behind a girl in her gear with her helmet reading her motorcycle
     manual – the facing couple is reading Astounding Science Fiction
     (he looks like he should be a biker) & the Readers Digest Book of
     Strange Love Stories, Amazing Facts (she looks like her long white
     fingernails) a happy marriage, why not

let the child be
let's us become

it's always a good time to slip under the bridge
why didn't I think of that

we wake
(we must have turned over)
facing the way

I dig in my back to find my keys & I put them bag in my pocket
it takes them all to get myself home

untitled

I was the book
'til I finished

I was thinking
'til I heard you

I was hiding
'til I saw you

THE CANAMAMA LECTURES

attention spanner

Every one of us makes this one burnt pot of coffee. We are indifferent only when we don't know each other, like some audience that never meets itself. Don't read for more than less without taking care of where you are & who's there with you, or we'll burn the coffee.

theme to be spoken in the amateur human voice

END SQUARE RULE
'Everything we do is to change this world.' (Fletcher Copp)

'reaching over fascism' (Greg Jupiter)

'I'm an American artist & I have no guilt.' (Patti Smith)

'I'm a Canadian artist & I have no quilt.' (Kate van Dusen)

'The major issue facing artists now is self-censorship.' (Robert Filliou)

'one third of a million Canadians have been jailed by the Ministry of
   Love narcotics squads.' (D. Facto)

'Bad art
'is the irresponsible impersonal lies
'of the slaves
'of the propaganda advertising education & media industries.'
   (Sandy Footing)

'As speech itself once was
'poetry is pulled from the flames of the unspeakable.
'Poetry is the freedom of speech.' (Slim Flower)

'Remind me to refuse the Governor General's Award.' (Gerald
   Gilbert)

the spoken world

   English & French are 2 of the major international languages of imperi-
alism, & as such they are here to stay. Naturally they are at war with each
other, but they're as cosy together as an apple core in an empty cigarette
package – the Canadian sandwich. The redistribution of power & wealth
in this country will be at the expense of French & English language & cul-
ture. We will create a Canadian language & culture free from U.S. &
European domination by encouraging the dozens – hundreds? – of indi-
ginous & immigrant languages being thought in, if not spoken in, all over
our north quarter of the world. At present these languages are being des-
troyed, as they were in the U.S.A., or they are used as instruments of
alienation, to keep different cultures apart, as in Europe. I suggest that
schools be required to teach the home languages of their students, & that
students learn at least one language other than French & English. The
Native languages speak from the hearts of every place in this land. The
"foreign" languages are the family ties we have with every place in the
rest of the world. At present, we don't know our own languages. So we
have nothing to say. All we can do is listen to ourselves being had, on
every front, especially the 49th Parallel. Remember, the next time you
tune in (or turn in) to the nuclear sell from the U.S.A. or the U.K. or
France ('... & here's Johnny!') – remember: 'All great world-shaking
events have been brought about not by written matter but by the spoken

word!' as Hitler proved, & said. Let's talk ourselves into Canada.

provincial pitch

There is a pitch of voice which every Province is accustomed to use in local & national conversation, which forms a kind of key note, & from which ethnic groups and geographical regions requiring to be distinguished, either rise or fall. This pitch of voice is different in different provinces, but always the same in the same province, & is one of the characteristics by which the voice of one province is known from that of another. On that provincial pitch of voice the tones in spontaneous language are provincial; but if any other pitch of voice be adopted locally or nationally, it is very difficult to retain the provincial inflections of the voice; & the enunciation becomes in that case constrained & unprovincial. It is of much importance, therefore, in local & national speaking to retain this provincial pitch of voice, & to add to it the necessary degree of force without altering it. Further, it will be found that it is easy to rise to this provincial pitch of voice from a lower pitch, but exceedingly difficult to come down to it, if a higher pitch has been once adopted. An obvious rule is suggested by this observation, for provinces who have occasion to address their localities or the nation, namely, to commence at as low a pitch as they can render audible; for, as they proceed, they will gradually rise to their provincial pitch, & thus retain possession of their provincial inflections; whereas, if they commence too high, they will find it scarcely possible to come down to their provincial pitch, & their manner will be unconvincing, either smart-allecky local, or grimly national.

can a Canadian live stoned?

Canadians are rather frequently found imprisoned in coal & stones; & people have often been inclined to jump to the conclusion that the Canadians had been imprisoned ever since the coal or stone was laid down, as if Canadians had therefore an extraordinary power of living for hundreds or millions of years without food & air. It is, of course, not true. Noncanadians could not believe that Canadians had any such remarkable vitality, & experiments in the Canadian consciousness proved that Canadians die within a year if deprived of both air & food, & that they cannot live two years without air even if given plenty of food. The Canadians that are found in holes in stones & coal from which they cannot escape must have crept in through some crevice when they were quite small, & have found enough food to make them too big to creep out again. With a little air & a few snowballs to eat they might live a few years, but certainly not longer than unstoned people, & never, of course, for centuries.

domestic animals

All our domesticated animals once lived the independent life of wild creatures, maintaining the struggle for existence alone by their own powers of self-preservation.

The man & the woman were domesticated thousands of years ago, probably before there was any history, & while the pussycat was still a savage. The man is believed to have been at first a kind of louse, preying perhaps in packs upon the less aggressive wild animals of the forest & the open plain. He has been greatly changed by his long association with pussycats, & has developed traits which seem to be quite feline, such as his evident pleasure in being praised. Indeed, in his warm response to the affection of his master, & his faithfulness even in adversity, he displays qualities only too rare among pussycats. In earlier ages the man was no doubt of great service to pussycats in safeguarding them against such enemies as hunger & rain.

The woman retains more of the original savage characteristics of her wild ancestors, a kind of oyster, than does the man. The woman has done considerable service in ridding pussycats of enemies such as fleas & kittens.

In these days, however, men & women are in general not so necessary to pussycats. Indeed, in many communities, people are far too numerous. They destroy large numbers of each other, & it is probable that they often carry the germs of infectious diseases in their frequent visits from house to house.

Domestic children are descended from the wild novelists which once roamed the plains. During many generations they have contributed largely, whether in love or under threat of punishment, to supplying the needs of the tribes & nations of pussycats who domesticated or adopted them. The child has done an immense amount of work for pussycats – thinking up names for them, cleaning out their litter boxes, & making them look smart.

Many breeds of children have been developed in different parts of the world. Some breeds have been specially adapted for crying; others have been bred chiefly for practicing on musical instruments.

The senior citizen was originally a power-hungry snail, active & sure-footed, able to slide from cliff to cliff, blazing trails through the wilderness since slime began. Wild senior citizens are still found in politics in both hemispheres. Senior citizens formed a large part of the wealth of the pastoral tribes of pussycats in Asia ages ago. In cold-temperate countries their words are indispensible for wisdom & their silence forms a large part of a pussycat's peace.

the very idea

We are each present for about half a century. There are only 20,000 half-centuries in the past 1,000,000 years. Human history is a city smaller than Prince Rupert. Save your hunger for something to eat. Save your money for something free. There are 1000 languages being spoken in the world today & each is something you can save your breath in. The movies like Star Wars & the things shot into the sky like the probe with the phonograph record saying, 'We're coming to get you!' are slower than sound. To speed time up, to go faster than light, to reach any place else, is quite a different move, in space, in peace.

SOUND IS IN ACCORD WITH LIGHT

DO		THE		THE
NO		BEG		AT
THING		IN		END
WITH		IN		ANT
THE		A		PUTS
TIME		HAND		THE
OF		THE		JUMP
LIST		END		BACK
END		A		UP
IN	MAN	FOOT	I	AFT
TO	A	OR	READ	HER
THE	M	THE	MIND	HIS
RE	U	O	BARE	TALE
CHORD	S	THERE	WHAT	KNOCKS
BY	H	A	I	IT
JOHN	R	WAY	SAY	BACK
CAGE	O	ROUND	WHEN	DOWN
	O		I	
	M		FOR	
	MU		GET	
	SH		WHAT	
	RO		I	
	OM		MEAN	
	MUSH		IS	
	ROOM		THE	
	SLUG		RAIN	

SEE

THE

MOUNT

EYES

WAIT

WHILE

I

FINI

SHED

THE   I   STAND   SOME

POEM   FOR   DING   DAYS

THEN   GET   OFF   I

THEY   WHAT   THERE   FEEL

TAKE   I   IN   CONE

ART   SAY   THE   TENT

A   WHEN   AIR   FOR

WAY   I   HERE   ME

           REACH   TO

           MY   SEE

           HEAR   SOME

           WHAT   OR

           I   NONE

           MEAN   OF

           IS   IT

           THE   IS

           HERE   FREE

I

CAN

HEAR

THE

MUSE

HIC

UP

CLEAR

EAR

I

COULD

NOT

DO

IT

TO

THE

CAT

WITH

THE   COME

HAM   POSED

MER   ON

RING   AN

IN   OR

HIS   RANGE

HEAD   FLY

START   CARD

                     BY

                     A

                     TWO

                     BIT

                     BUS

                     PASS

                     EN

                     GER

                     E

LET

TEAR

THE

SOUND

BE

IT

SELF

LET

IT

SELF

BE

THE

SOUND

LET

SELF

BE

SOUND

IME
A
LIT
ISLE
PO
ET
TALL
&
THIN
O

CRUNCH
YOU
SCORE
&
HOW
DO
YOU
DO
IT
SOUNDS

JOHN   PEN   TRY   LIKE   THE
SANG   ME   IT   YOU   FIRE
ME   UP   OUT   EAT   DROVE
HOW   &   ON   THE   BY
TO   FILL   YOUR   CORE   THE
LOOK   ME   SELF   &   EARTH
AWE   IN   FIRST   MORE   TURNED
WAY   STARE   ON
FROM   AT   THE
THE   AN   WHAT
SEA   EYE   TURNED
QUENCH   LASHED   IN
CHING   TO   TO
MY   A   AIR
THIRST   STAR   THE
FOR   AIR   LAWN
SAND   CASE   DRY

BOTTOM LINES

I thought you said aspirin

room smelt of socks burntoast & camels
I was on page 441 of the good book Gravity's Rainbow
it leant on my black or blue cords
from the orange peel leatherette armchair
& pisst beer all the way from here to Hallowe'en
explaining how
if I go to the moon with her
I should wear my warm sweater

the Europe

the you rope

Popes 2
Dodgers 0

strike now
ball later

drinkdrinkdrink
that's better

I don't mind the music
so long as it changes

the coffee has a cop at the counter

I keep glancing in return to the waitress
that I don't want more beer
it's her I'm looking to

but never fear
it's me I see

a neat scotch in the rest of the glass
& here's to

the coast is clear

growing up BC

the early in life flavour of raincoat Vancouver
morning coffee breaks

new friends & newspapers
elbow to elbow at the counter

(I'm sure I just heard her say
'Legally, I can screw anybody')

it's the early 50s
the gov't is selling the Columbia river to Billy Graham

it's the late 70s
the papers still haven't figured it out

I take the cap off my thinking pen
& stab the donut hole like this

they'd have nothing to do
without us to do it to

dolly mountain

the kid's doll
needs the kid

I need sleeping
sing to me

I need waking
talk to me

we need the future
poetry better not be late again

the 80s are coming
the kids are getting desperate

when the mountain comes to save us
it's more than we need

the rhythm changes suddenly
everyone falls over

loose talk

the children come to me to learn poetry
& I tell them to brush their teeth

the photos I take turn out better than I do
the tv set sits on a crate marked 'lye water'

my upper partial broke in two a couple weeks ago
hence the title & thither the autumn

the world is falling on me & at the last moment
there's nothing I can do but hide inside my ribs

I don't want you or you or you
I want you & you & you

read a sound & hear a sight
tonight is not alone tonight

may please I be excused from the paper now
it was a very good poem thank you

the hold

just enough to keep the page open to
the place we used
to live

in out of the
the time since
since when

did I lose you
I lost you
then

it was just last night
for a dream
I held

you in my eyes
you fell down in your laughter
you pulled me after

I loved you
and it was me
and we are gone

paper roots

can I take it
what do I know about anything but this
what does a raccoon seeing a bear see
can I give it

this is a net for words

I went to the window to watch the light grow
while I was there it brushed my hair

say it with slugs

may the permanent continuous high-energy buddhist find a door
    on his way out

I had a normal day last week

a man meets a friend in the pouring rain
they sit on a bench, take off their hats & talk
'where did I learn to get wet like this' he asks
'curiosity killed the u in curious' the friend replies

pretty soon the bus goes by

marking time

'I should have started earlier,' I said, turning off the know-it-all. I've
developed a leer paying attention to all that used news. I squeezed
myself a shot of Orafix & stared at a cigarette instead. I couldn't remem-
ber putting it out. I tried to come to think of it. I closed my eyes & grew
breasts but they weren't mine. I slipped them back to her before she
noticed. So many of her. So much for her. & nothing for me. I didn't go
anywhere. I'm still here. Writing again. The clock strikes out. I should
have stopped earlier. I'll go away & come back. It worked. Now I did
start earlier. Move up, make room for everybody – this may be what
you've been waiting for. In my time this is poetry, something to the pur-
pose, à propos, après prose. 'Hows about a little poem for the road?'
You're not going anywhere. 'Aw, c'mon – something for the little lady,
something that rhymes....' Ok: THE WORKER HAS A RIGHT TO THE
STRIKE / THE CITIZEN HAS A RIGHT TO THE REVOLUTION. The
waitress looked down at me & my little black notebook & asked if it's my
bible. I just tapped my head & said, 'It's things to do.' She said (& I lie, it
was a fortune in an xmas cracker – no offence, Billy) 'The great pleasure
in life is doing what people say you cannot do.' The trick in eating a jam
poem is licking your sticky thinkers – jam as in jazz & jam as in felt,
pressed together & wiped right off the air. Love is a pain in the ask. I can't
stop to say everything – I'm saying this so everything can start. Full
ahead & nobody to it, the peacock jiggling his tail-monsters faster than
the eye can think of us. Hey, Billy Shakespeare, I couldn't sell that lovely

little leather-bound edition of your sonnets to any Vancouver bookstore today. You've had a free ride long enough, Billy. Get out & join the walking class. Don't be coy, be coiled, like a snake, like exactly the right number of clothespegs, & don't worry about being too good for Canadian literature, the happy hooker has something to be happy about, the modest poet has something to be modest about. Nothing anyone can do will make it all worthwhile – suffering belongs to everyone. The first ring sounds like the second & the last ring never comes. Just stand out there, on the grass, holding on. If you think this is a spectator sport watch out, the rain will solve all your paper problems. Chew planet brittle. The price of admission rises the later you get here. Wealth warning: no amount of paper is enough. Our wings are clipped to fly fast – let's catch that light! Another month bites the mouth that feeds it. The oscillators are waiting up for us. You know what to say & so shut up & say it. Sink your teeth into it. Draw sleep, pull it out & forget yourself. Do you laugh much? Remember yourself. Go west, old night. Now I did stop earlier.

thing

MY THINGS – MY THINGS

MY NOTEBOOK EMPTIES ME
MY BAG DRAGS ME
MY BOOTS LEAK ME
MY DINNER EATS ME

NO-ONE WILL UNDERSTAND – MY THINGS

MY MANNERS BETRAY ME
MY RENT TEARS ME
MY BENT BENT-OAK SWIVEL-CHAIR TWISTS ME
MY TEETH ROT ME

THE LAST OF MY DOZEN YELLOW PENCILS

MY RUG TRACKS ME
MY PHOTOGRAPHS SILENCE ME
MY WRITING FORGETS ME
MY SWEATER SWEATS ME

THE TROUBLES THAT I CAN'T DO WITHOUT

MY DREAMS LEAP ME
MY ROOM ASSUMES ME
MY PAST GROWS ME
MY FUTURE KNOWS ME

MY THINGS – MY THINGS

MY WINDOWS HIDE ME
MY BOOKS DECIDE ME
MY THINGS INFEST ME
MY THINGS DIGEST ME

3 views of North Van for Snow White

such a day
reflections show the other way

sun shines down
the mountain town

the dark spills
the light fills

behold

skating with
without skates

the face of life
has frozen yellow hair blowing in her eyes

& a red barrette
& a green barrette

I don't mind winning her fingers
she doesn't mind losing my gloves

small old songs
light on us

the blackbirds fit right into the dazzle & hide there
I wake first for once

same
day

turning myself in

After weeks of ice, it started to rain in Vancouver as soon as I got the
wax cleaned out my ears. It turns out that my MD for the past 14 years
was a shrink, but he's moved on to his Waterloo. If Canada's national
cold sweat had kept on much longer I was going to cancel my annual trip
onto Toronto, but I knew this morning when the letter came, crossing
mine over Big Suck Lake, Saskatchewan, each writing the other as soon
as the new year was initialed, that I could go & buy that fire, that after all I
fell in love & held her head in my hands & kissed her breast there long
before I ever spoke. I'm a mother's son & I will go see for myself, one
more time, one less winter. Ah, but who will play that very first day &
who will be me & say, 'So why talk talk talk, when one walk around the
town, delivering the month to the year, for sure, for now, for all I know,
does it.'

reading music

I think she likes me perched here
on the bough of her sight

here now
n.o.w. here

she plays the bow
I plays the arrow

stop the band
I want to get hungry

start the band
I want some other time

the likes of me quiver
the bow lets me go

the bough breaks
the band falls

the neck's table

it's going to rain
'but it *is* raining'
I know *that*
that was happening before we walked in

quick
take a sniff of cucumber

light an Export A like a straight Canadian
Camels blended with sugar bent America

Canada
Lost
Geese
Lagoon

thank here
we're there

classical joint

until I saw the movie
I thought it was me

would you be listening
if I wasn't talking

there you are
& I'm not even here

I cruise by outside
barely see in

I am not the recording
you are not the fare

this is live
& other minor traditions

this is going home alone
it was the world

Rohan's

I danced in my violet cowboy shirt
to Rose of San Antone

Jack gave me an Irish coffee for the New Year
& said the little stitches in the checks are scorpions
like the ones on Mexican pants that discourage pickpockets

it's a good shirt
the scorpions crackle when I take my sweater off it
nobody can touch me when they really get moving

*

I'm about due for a milky mama

lead me
follow me
dance all over me

I'll stay up later in my life
do a little more standing
a little less stalking

learn some new walks

some words you don't say
& you don't forget
about her

o Jack

I wanna land
like a speck of shit
in a bucket of cream

neat trick

The only place open. An hour's walk back downtown from Kits. 2 to 3 a.m. Small chili, pre-buttered bun, a sty of coffee, 90 cents. Sit in the middle, at the edge of it. Light her cigarette. She sat down & tore a little yellow book to bits & dropped them disgustedly into the bin. The never has bin. It didn't bother me but it did get to me. I didn't say anything to anybody. When I whipped out my Zippo, her face was close & in profile. She was somewhere nearby. My eyes but not hers. I wanted to brush her hair. She picked up a long & broken corner of plate glass mirror & looked about in it, around out of it, holding it as a dagger in her small hand. The easy-gone guy there, he kept talking, '... yeah I love you, you love me eh, we're gonna get that farm & have 8 kids, so let's start right now!' When they got back from the can, the come easy guy at the table, who wasn't really not talking, said, 'Where's your glasses?' & his jaw moved uneasily, 'Where's my glasses – maybe I left them ...?' Reaching. The unspoken answer pointed at them on the table & they were in his hands before he knew it.

privacy

I got some meat inside
he don't sleep nights
nothing's moving in on him!

I'm in the way
I'm his skin
& I'm moving out on you

just as easy as knowing the story
& turning down the sound

goodbye
from mister meat & I

hello
you know you never know

I never closed
you never opened

BOOTS

they got so good at making their new boots
that I can't afford them anymore
so I wear my old boots, or yours, or theirs
as long as my feet, or longer
maybe 2 years, with summers off
& running but usually I walk
the time it takes to keep fit
in sandals that last forever
so I get there soon enough

a love letter wouldn't take long enough to write tonight
I've tamed the cat & come to bed instead
in cold bare feet & sleepy head

*

the uppers on my service boots are cracked through
but the skies are clear today
& the old doctor was right
early for love is as good as waiting for rain
any old boots will do
I might as well get dressed

I've emptied the pipe
that's why the pipe is empty

the heels are too high for walking in my other boots
my just in (lower) case wellingtons
they're saving me for idling in
as I remember it, they leak too

you said noon & it's nearly 2

maybe a million people are listening
maybe not
maybe I'm alone

*

boot eats fute
gude food

silent h
earing you

feet eat up the miles
good fould

I'm not
as far behind as I thought

take
a look

give it
back

nearly near
enough for jazz

what I thought when you didn't show up was

1 just as well
2 I can't afford this $2.50 for a beer & busfare
3 our love life is a waste of time I'm pleased you noticed
4 I never let on but I love myself
5 I suppose you know what you're doing
6 I wonder what the late movie is
7 on my way home I suppose I'll stop in at the Cecil
8 it's the dead air space that insulates
9 how come we have such bright afternoons with the kids
      but I can't get started with you
10 there's always one of us not kissing back
11 I'm sorry I brought the subject up
12 twelve & thirteen & fourteen
13 thirteen & fourteen
14 fourteen & evermore will be so, gringo

VALENTINE

PUCK SEX
fucking your face off

PUNK SEX
fuck the 70s

SUCK SEX
blind fuck

SOAKA SOULA SEX
fuck of the month club

FOOD SEX
fuck on the cob

WORK SEX
fuckalong

FAST SEX
fucked

SOUND BUSINESS SEX
fuck you

DRIP DRY POLITICAL SEX
infucking

PURE RELIGIOUS SEX
heaven can't fuck

HARD MUSICAL SEX
fuck up

HARD LITERARY SEX
fuck sitting

EASY LITERARY SEX
fuck water

EASY MUSICAL SEX
fuck air

CANADIAN SEX
defuckto

WEST COAST SEX
fuck forward

PRAIRIE SEX
fuck it

ONTARIO SEX
fuck on

QUEBEC SEX
indefucktable

MARITIME SEX
refuck

ARCTIC SEX
born to fuck

U.S. SEX
polyfuck

TAKE-OUT SEX
fuck city

LOTO SEX
fuckily

FAMILY SEX
sleepfucking

BAD SEX
fuck off

GOOD SEX
oh fuck

LOVE SEX
fuck

BABY SEX
little fucker

CHILD SEX
stayfree minifuck

TEEN SEX
fucktime

ADULT SEX
for fuck sake

SENIOR CITIZEN SEX
fuck dying

ANIMAL SEX
hushfucking

CANADIAN SEX II
fuck all

MALE SEX
plugfuck

FEMALE SEX
fuck it to me

GAY SEX
artfuck

LIBERATED SEX
fuck sex

DRUNKEN SEX
fuck who

STONED SEX
fuck me

PERVERTED SEX
styrofuck

JET SEX
flying fuck

MULTI-NATIONAL CORPORATE SEX
deathfuck

UNMARRIED SEX
fuckaround

MARRIED SEX
3 square fucks a day

EASY ART SEX
fuck & tell

HARD ART SEX
show & fuck

NORMAL SEX

*

there's

the feel
you'd free

your life
for more

time
some

one to
touch you

all
small

ever
over

up against
once again

THE 1979 SPRING OPEN TOUR
OF THE CANADAS

Vancouver

I am reminded of myself
by the familiar sound of the tap

cap in mouth
what could be plainer

Sherlock Homeless
Consulting Poet

gave individual initiative leading to personal success up
for lent if you want to borrow it

when I wake raw it's not because the alarm went off
it's because I got to sleep done

smooth morning
sea weather & all

liver & onion

I don't want dessert
I've paid enough for this table already
so much for so little

I don't want to sit right down & write myself a letter

how come there isn't a cookbook for what I eat?

I'm gonna tour the country for 6 weeks
& find out what I'm supposed to be writing about
I leave Sunday
it's all so tenuous

no-one else tries to make a living at it

I'm up to here in the Ovaltine
looking for someone to drink?
maybe I'm talk sick

the shiny surface of the dark brown HP sauce on the plate is like
    the skin of a wet slug
the food goes out in the order it came in

I read in the Nut & Dick yesterday that the brain is a sex organ

I get to go out in the cold night now knowing what good is for

this is not the only poem you need to hear this year
this is not the poem you always hoped would be written

ready or not

you can't stand driving just like some people can't stand tv
you give your bike to a tree
you walk as far as you can see

when you take a bus across the continent you get to stand on the actual
    ground every 3 hours or so & whatever else it takes to be anywhere
    it takes that first, so no matter how crude & uncomfortable being
    thousands of Canadians travelling thousands of miles by bus can
    be, it sure beats flying
the train is just the best possible plane

time does not live by man alone

this is the first time many of these meanings have met

your arrival is not an interruption
your departure brings no relief

the phone has the ring of belief
but it too leaves you in the same place which you want to move off

from moment to moment
you pick it up & add it to the book

the book is a wheel
in the act of understanding it you are the ground

Vancouver grey? Hound Edmonton.

shut up & listen
to the road to
the truth is
it's abroad in the land tonight

'all the political parties are on a collusion course' says Ben Metcalfe,
    commenting that Parliament never debates foreign affairs or the
    uranium industry

take your time
I've got mine

fuck! I woke up at Hope & had 2 coffee & nothing to read
so this will have to do

every 2nd story in the local paper is a traffic crime
every 2nd story in the local paper is about a traffic crime

do you just want talk about what happened
5 years ago today?
10 25 50 100 10000 50000
that's what talk is talking about
years ago today

at dinner we talked about trying to fly
Taki says 'study the birds
'they start on the ground & work up from there
'birds don't jump out windows'
Gordon says 'if you land on your face don't survive'
George was so quiet he was sick

the lights are on in the tunnels
don't tell me the mountains are afraid of the dark!
I'll tell you

does Boston Bar have a hockey team?

I think the turns indicate the signals
relativity speaking

I've been up so long
it seems like, well
like it's
down to me
nobody else even awake

prepare to meet thy dream

your sleep is showing
that pun
that meant
that
as well
as this
deep

Kam
loops
thru
tru
dawn
nine
pine
still
fine

so far
so near

living in the world like I can afford these long distances
you think I'm any richer inside than outside?
I can barely afford these Mexican jeans but they've such an antique
    droop that with

my old pinstripe twobreasted Cambridge jacket
& my abovecontempt boots
& my BR longsleeve patentlover vest

get thee behind me, Jasper!

& yes
my nest of scorpions shirt
my pindot navelblue shirt too
my brotherofpearl warmerthanthou
one oneholedadjustable openwide elastic beltinthemiddle
my six married socks
my colourdecoded underwear
my gravityfeed raincoat
my surviving scarf
my ears popping
my bulletproof silk neckerchief
all my permanent loans
my ten little fingerbags
my GO WITH THE GRAIN beershirt
my robinshood green smokingshirt
my available toque
my spyintheeye trilby banded by a wealth of belief in the first thing
    you see
my fatherofpearl tie
& my fourteen pockets of ice

I bring
spring

Edmonton poems is

asking the audience what it wants to know
getting to politics by way of dreams
Ukrainia
the guys bullying the boy who's friends with girls
everything in the supermarket in the same place as in mine
every wasted barrel of oil someone's long cold winter someday just so
    we can be covered all over by the sweet violence of money

throwing out the half you read & keeping the half you heard
never waiting for it to be over
liking you with all my art, depth of art, art's length
the smell of the full moon
a downtown airport
watching our eyes change the wind
settling for best
Highway 2 to Calgary on fire

Calgary poems is

it was a 3-Vladimir reading I mean
Calgary is bigger than Alberta I mean
Calgary is a flash in the panic I mean
you can do what you can in Calgary I mean
but in Alberta you gotta do what you got I mean
peace is bigger than war I mean
the poem is bigger than the story I mean
the drunks begging at the front door of the Glenbow Museum & the
    top floor collection of weapons & the art in the middle of the war are
    smaller than the ... the ... I mean ...
the vision, the way you see, see even this I mean
Calgary makes me younger than any other city I mean
open faced I mean
Calgary has critical mass I mean
Alberta has an uncritical mask I mean
57% voted the Cons into 90% of the seats I mean
you mean a lot to me I mean
you expect poetry

60 hours to Montreal

the weather happens Sunday afternoon an hour east of Calgary
the cattle are standing around as if they don't get the joke
but the road is breaking up here
& there, a banana jumps out of its skin with a sneeze
this kiss stops all the way to let the real cross, singing

the clouds are having pressed land for lunch
kids are flashing between kites & hilltops
a few patches of wise old snow sneaking up from below for a final look
a bean from the third to last spoon of last night's chili gives a friendly
    fart to cushion the dream of the girl curled on the armrest up ahead
    on the bus of us
oil wells pumping away at memory
the bus that passeth all our undertakings

pay as you leave

medicine
a hat

5 o'clock
a shadow

enter
a prize

no hot food in the bus depot so I keep my cool
for a walk around the block
it makes sense
sober
Christian Dollars & Cents

(a cent costs 2 to mint
cities are expensive too
but they are a more efficient way to use up the world than wars
a city is a walk there
compared to a war

of silence

the prize
of surprise

what war? the one you take the medicine for)

Exit
alone

zombie

    Karen Ann Quinlan lies unfocussed in a sunny hospital room, with only liquid nutrients seasoned with antibiotics & served with a prayer & rock 'n' roll on the radio, so maybe The Top Ten is the way through to her

        I bet your shit
        is lily white

        I bet your eyes
        are hard as ice

        I bet you're in
        Karen Ann

        you're the future's twin
        Karen Ann

        the Devil is a fan
        of yours Karen Ann

        your life is his plan
        for us all Karen Ann

        take a stand
        & die Karen Ann

cracks

I'm an alcoholic,' he says, but I'm already giving him his 35 cents &
swallowing a bran muffin & coffee & opening a pack of fuckin' A's &
circling in the rain outside today around the bus depot, looking for a
place to light a spliff for the next 200 km of zoo
the trees & the rocks are watching you
pluck the lid off the bend in the road the coffee flies around moistening
the air in here
I kept being woken by the cracking of lip
with a sound like the painted-out graffiti on the Canadian Shield
I scored a rear seat triple in Calgary yesterday aft & it'll last at least
until Sudbury tomorrow noon
I'm perched here behind the rear wheels
this tale is cracking right along
here, this'll crack you up – I wasn't just dodging panhandlers while I
was looking for a place in Kenora to light up, I was keeping the cover
on at least one other furtive smoke-ring, a couple of kids sending out a
long lazy cloud of green signal that I actually saw blowing intact
around the corner
'I'll cover for you,' he said unto me, spreading himself out around the
dime & quarter (freely passing money around is also illegal) & we
shook hands forever
the coins flipping me around the corner where the smoke come from &
I kept rolling upwind, meeting my own easy 7 puffs on the way back &
landing heads up
I hope this isn't too old for you, this final issue of Howard the Duck on
the comic racks now, that he was one of the great 40 cent wise-crackers
and lit will be a little less marvelous without him cracking up at this
speed we love at, is it all that it's cracked up to be, when (as Howard
the Egg used to say) you've 'reached the Himalayan Hilton as far as
last resorts go!')
I hear faintly that China is gonna let tourists in to finish off Tibet
Dryden Ontario
a flood of mud
& snow to go

Thunder Bay

THUNDER BABY
MID CANADA VACUUM
ST. JOHN NEEDS NURSES
MOOSE HOME
GIANT TIRE
POETS DO IT ... FOR NOTHING
COSMO VOX
THE CLASS MENAGERIE
CROOK'S PHARMACY
DRIVE YOUR MERC / DON'T DRINK IT

that was one-a-them ten-line metric sonnets

Hey man, can you find any more poetry on that radio? I sure could use some more poetry.

What do you like?

Oh you know, something that moves right – I like it when it moves real *real* fast, so that it starts to pulse, bend, smooth – all the writer's got to do is make the corners, hit the directions straight on – I like the curves.

You must be standing a long way back.

That's where it can put you all right. But like I say, there's nothing like the driver's seat, get in there behind that voice! I read, myself, a little, you know, but I still can't hear as much as just listening – actively – it's a real test of how relaxed your attention can be. What's being said starts in the music and it only makes sense when you kind of dance to it – it doesn't have to rhyme or anything – shit, it can be Phone Book!

Yeah, I can always tell – oboy! – as soon as it's music!

Yeah but – you listen *to* them musicks all right – but you hear the language, what's being said, & what you're thinking about it – the poem is only a third or a quarter of what you're in to, & you have plenty of space to be really tough & critical, especially if the poem is smart to begin with – you listen *through* the music & you're all there & you can bring what you're thinking but it doesn't slow you down because the poetry starts hitting *everything* you know – everything comes into play, in the place between your mind & the poet's – it's the way I set up my day – & you don't have to worry about bad poems, they're good for a laugh & a cry, just don't swallow 'em – for me, getting into a poem is like seeing what my mind's made of – you know you never actually hear silence, eh? – there's always the heart & the nerves & the world buzzing – but then you can, in these parts of the room that are *silent* – like all of a sudden there's nothing – of course this is the fresh poem I'm talking about, there's a lot of stale doggerel & caterwauling, the advertising & the news ...

... & the bullshit! Poesy is where they grows it, eh.

Yeah, you gotta let it be nonsense, man, 'cause that's what the language first sounded like to us – each poem is learning all over again – when you write it or read it or however you hear it – you don't have to like the poet or yourself even, to meet what's being said – & the poem is an opportunity to sort out what's important – I trust that – that's the tune.

I only wish it were true.

Me too. There's only a few thousand poets in the whole country worth listening to.

we slept for joy

all that snow on the ground
didn't fall off all those birches
did it?

was all that ice

fitting right around the curves of La Rivière Veuve
bespoke?

we slept where we fell
waking all in one peaceful rest of winter
no question

Québec Immigration

HALT – WHO GOES THERE?
SLUG IN THE BOX

WHAT HAVE YOU SEEN?
THE RED DIRT STREETS OF MATTAWA

WHAT DID YOU THERE?
I LEFT MY HAT & SCARF ON A CHAIR IN PEMBROKE

HOW ARE WE GONNA TELL YOU FROM LAST YEAR?
THEY'RE GONNA SEND THE BAND ON

CONTRABAND!
HATBAND

PASSWORD?
VIVE MAGGIE TRUDEAU LIBRE!

THE LATEST GOVERNOR-GENERAL JOKE?
I WOULDN'T WANT TO BE IN HIS REVOLUTION

Montréal poems is

2 real strawberries on the cheesecake
a really local motive

real easy on the people

real hard on the dogs

real Downtown Saturday Night
real soot landing on the paper

really broke & really me
really getting it on at the gig

real time at my feet
real forgetful of Ontario

surreal driving on the road
real dirty anglo lyrics on franco radio disco

unreal cold & no fair
really floored & no chair

a real handful of mountain
a real mountainful of river

who goes there

clue: he taught all the Canadian poets who needed teaching

federal infection

Trudeau means false money
everything Joseph Clark says is a vast distraction

as for Ed Broadbent
let's leave social democracy out of this
this traitor of the mouth club

history has instructed me to say:
GRIT BIG SHIT POURED THROUGH TORY SMALL BORE SOUND LIKE SOCIALISM
    FARTING

history has a Chinese accent

Toronto poems is

there's an easy way to write this
there's a Book Writer's Reception at the Park Plaza, to rest my legs on
    the way, & I'm the only one I see writing
there's a moratorium on public marijuana smoking until everyone's
    made a way lot more money
there's an embarrassed pause, all the way from the kid's balloon
    popping down to the last storm of the winter
there's a lot of tweed in the way
there's a long way to temporary
there's a point in which the poem gets out of the way

taking all afternoon to do right what someone could do wrong
    in half an hour
white hound lane
to reach your own
if the food weren't so good I'd have talked more
buying into instead of falling into
the writers are so serious you'd think they run the country
the artists are so serious you'd think they run the city
everyone so serious you'd think they run & hid here
I know more people here than anywhere else, not counting Vancouver
    as usual
as fast as Asparagus in April
my scruffier-than-thou attitude this year
the lushes are still hanging the visionaries
loose as a Calgary gypsy in Toronto traffic
I'll leave you the moon full
I brought the winter back to the best April snow in 139 years
    & nobody wants it
as the cabby said, 'People work like hell here, can't stop, then on
    weekends a couple of drinks & blotto!'

federal erection

for one clear moment I couldn't find the CN Space Syringe
the habits some people put up with
just to remind them what hit them

I'm glad to see

that big wind again
I knew it when it was a gust
& I'd lie in my cot in the attic with the light on & watch it
hit bend & fill the cedar roof like it would a sail
while the whale's tooth on the shelf made me small
& the iron pirates in the bottle made me a fool

the only secrets I have left are my own

Randy found me the green strides I left here 30 years ago
they were drapes then
now they're pegged just above my boots
now I can wash my jeans & my other greens when I get to Regina
which reminds me
I banged my nose on the Queen Mother
cafe door
the peanut butter banana sandwich was so engrossing
it stuck me to the last smoking seat on the bus
Good Friday the 13th is 37 hours long
lose a night here
gain a day there
I realize this isn't everybody's story
some people are only going to Blind River

the whole thing

the one-carrot sun
dangles just over the hill
the hill to the west

dear dire

a pleasant change
a sleep with 47 strangers
off & on
Sudbury to Thunder Bay
you snow
I rain
we fog
they were lightning the horizons of Lake Superior
hot slime
diesel down the highway
Wawa for breakfast
sleep in 47 impositions
wake only to spot the rock I missed coming
passenger patience
preparing for prairie

still life

the girl across the aisle has *Gerald* tatooed on the back of her left hand
 & the ground is whiter than the sky
the denim cops over there are smoking firecrackers & Jesus is in hell by
 now but we're still two hours from Kenora
the telephone poles go all the way back to Queen Street so far & no
 matter how fast your operator drives the bus the trees stay ahead
people are suspicious of something writing us down & the woman
 beside me last night has read one book this year, about what
 happened to the people who let their leader name their town after

himself
when the Canada Council moves its offices from Ottawa to Inuvik
    maybe the artists in Toronto will relax & one way to make friends
    with folks in Ontario is to complain bitterly when they overcharge
    you
I'm not gonna bother going anywhere anymore until everyone drops
    what they thought they were developing for the past ten years &
    picks up on what we all started out in search of together
the wet snow on the soft ice on that little lake out there will support
    only the quickest of glances & poets – there's one on every bus
gradually, going west, coffee refills get freer, nights get shorter – by the
    second night I remember the nightmare as I wake to a field of horses
    – I give my back seat to the French girl warm in a red sequinned
    halter & I step onto the deck in Regina – seems solid
let go & let's see

Regina poems is

dump a load of Toronto into the river & have a coffee with an old
    friend, then go to the laundromat & sit outside the machines &
    everytime the front door of the place closes, my eyes close

on beast behaviour
the cat waits until she hears my eyes open before coming in
the cat & I have scratchy tongues
to keep our first clean
& our lust mean

the skies have it
it took 91 years to haul this much snow into the April sunshine
for my wonder of the world today
& such nice clean slush!

hologram –
what a picture!
what a wall!

SLUG SMASHES STAPLEGUN
BLOOD OUT

DRAWS FIRE

wester –
Goodbye God

you build a new police station
to hide the site of an old battle
you're asking for a long winter

oreginal material –
the hills of money
the nothing down town
the politics of what's left

ramblin' prose

Driver, '... & for the ladies, no streaking in the aisle please,' & on leaving Swift Current (home of the Swift Current Bottlers) he calls out, 'Everybody missing hold their hands up!' I've finally made up my mind – winter is over & I can take off my sweater, revealing my new flavour, salt & vinegar. Farewell, Grilled Cheese. This coach is restroom equipped / for your winds disgusting to 55 km/h. A sign at the bus station of NO PARKING FROM HERE WEST. All that tumbleweed piling up against all these towns. All destinations final. From morning snow to spring for lunch to afternoon dust, follow the bouncing bus. New grass in the ditches here, too late for this year's deer back by Regina, where the crows had an extra month of snow to grow their hungry egos against. I can't see any mountains with all this sky in the way. That 20 foot high microwave tower must be the shortest in the country.

Read this as lines of longitude, & when you find the one you like best, cut north on it & go see who's standing above all this width. Hop Ontario, skip the prairies, jump off BC. When the Alberta driver asks us for our attention, I miss the Saskatchewan driver – he gave us his. I think BC should join Saskatchewan. Alberta can have Manitoba. It sounds crazy, if you've been aiming west-east all your life – but north goes farther – & meets! – & what is more: is *who*.

There's an intriquing sign in Irvine that says ANTIGUES.

Last night's reading really showed the poem how much the audience knows.

The Alberta driver is ok – he's like Bruce Dern with a sense of humour. The Saskatchewan driver was like Ed Broadbent with an afro.

landscape

the LiTTLE hand between 4 & 5 and the bIg hand at 6
Calgary 63 km
the fields look wet
the sky looks blue
a tiny hairstroke of mud on the window
times 1000s & 1000s of blades of grass
I'm as near as a mirror to the finely drawn brows of the eyes asleep
    beside me
the last edge of old snow looks like a month ago
the roof & wall panels in the bus are cut from marble
everyone sitting around in all the talking
clutching purses
pursing lips
we all realize
we're all real eyes

the story

I was born here
I know how to wear a hat
I can keep it simple

why was everyone in Alberta wearing new clothes yesterday?

train through the time zone into BC from Edmonton & wake sitting in
    the side of PG
the side of the Nechako or Fraser Lake
or Mouse Mountain with its tales of this winter's drowned skidooers
& the famous guys sawmills sliced lengthwise
& angling your bore sample into the next claim
& building with logs so well a cat would just shove the whole house
& somebody getting a ticket out there on Hwy 16 for talking too fast
& a 60 cent endless coffee in the dining car
& her finally finishing the back of the vest she's been knitting since
    Montréal & she's never going back
& a little well-washed sunshine in my particular window
& Dave Barrett aint so easy-goin' & trustin' nowadays thanks
& all the clearing that's been done & gone in the 30 years since I last
    tried these many ties
& the clean air joke about having your breakfast before you go out
    downwind of the mill
& the hummingbirds that have come north on the geese
& we live on/next to nothing
                next to nothing

Hazelton poems is

a sweep of street

did anyone here see that mountain go up?

5 poets
a hand

listen for
three two
river

I haven't been so far away since I left

vista

so
this
is what is

i
see

Terrace poems is

spikes sticking out of
along the top of the goalpost
& the green grass field
of Sunday morning kids
shouting the kite into the blue sky
voices hammered through the future
where they stick out of the past
like the deep blue mountains of
everything all around us under
the snow that doesn't melt
the poetry we won't forget

there's green weather
& a lake nearby
my father dropped his glasses in

Spring flew in & beat me here
but it was my uncle Fred who built the airport

plan on winter

sidewalk
a $2 bill
not enough

feed the Skeena the highway

students
turn on a teacher today

Prince Rupert poems is

same place
except the back yard never used to stop
plus a crab cocktail at Smile's

swinging cedars
from green to yellow
over my size pines

the road past the sandpit's shorter
but just as steep
right over there I figured out plastic
& so much for school

the schools have changed everything
but where they are

the string is gone but not the line
from Ray's tincan phone to mine

& that's where I learned to read
& this is what I learned to write

I was tiny

it's the water

let's float through that again

a few Skeena Oolichans
for the benefit of
all the eagles

4 foot BC Ferry couches
for the benefit of
passengers who are a little short

a new moon
for the benefit of
the return home

a northwest coast of golden skunk cabbage
for the benefit of
long may it rain

a federal subsidy of $1.25 an ear this tour
for the benefit of
the best hearing a poem ever had

a little Tennessee branch
for the benefit of
the Inside Passage

an extra afternoon walking around Rupert
for the benefit of
a kid raised in Pacific Milk

a promise to come back & live
for the benefit of
next century

shipping out
for the benefit of
the doubt

I never missed Van one minute while I was away
for the benefit of
sure glad to get back

drinking Kavanaugh with the Red Queen
for the benefit of
the history of Terrace

islands in night
for the benefit of
insight

she woke 6 times in memory of what was said
for the benefit of
her sense of humour

a good fit
for the benefit of
the thought of it

there you are

me again
emerging from yet another weather

have a smoke
nothing rises from these ashes

if you think advertising doesn't work
watch the drunk young man find his style

the land tumble into the sea
with a splash of sunshine

the bags under the window slide ahead
as steadily as the waters slip behind

I slept with the green wool toque pulled over my eyes
& woke to my surprise in a chatter of passengers filling the view

the Haywires got on in Bella Bella
four more last legs home

perfectly satisfactory afternoon on the Sound
rolling with the shadow & dodging sunspots

this is not novel
this is a Canada

now that we know we're this far
let's keep in touch

hummingbirds don't need feet

almost all the stars
flat on

Campbell River's lights
a lace snake

you face me
as simply as that

speaking of waking in a golden haze

I got quite blown away
on deck there today

pall mellow

2 herons
Tsawwassen

happy go lucky

we, Charlie Chan & number true son, Van der Valk, Nick & Nora,
    Hercule, the commissaris & Gripstra & de Gier, Sam & Ellen, McGee
    & Reeee & G & G & G
disembark & vanish into the morning rush hour
slide under the neckskin of the Fraser
a
here let me soften up the world for ya
kinda
sunlit cherrycourse golfblossom sprinklersplashed day
& the bus rearends a rabbit lightly without actually touching her
it seems she's lost
so we pinch her behind along SW Marine & turn north up Cambie &
    then down
tulips beeping
barely bare nipples of snow left on the Lions
beside us a 3-car crash which reminds us of the elections
above us the mountain which reminds us of ourselves
& the mountain which minds out for us
& the mountain which doesn't mind us at all
home free
from Chinatown in

Vancouver poems is

QUESTIONS FROM THE FLOOR

1. Is that fog cloud smog or shroud above us all?
2. Are you the half who can't remember or the half who can't forget?
3. If we knew the news whose little game would it spoil?
4. Do you have any conception?
5. Why does Art hate the Canadians?
6. Do you always wear it on the left side?
7. What do the flowers say when the slug comes to play?

ANSWERS OFF THE WALL

1. drifting all wrong in dreamland
2. hip-semi-city-self-notize
3. it's one thing to win & everything to lose
4. just as soon as I get this mirror out of my face
5. he loves the Canadas
6. she saw me coming
7. may day may day

money

bone
ring on my finger

bell
ring around my neck

when the time came
the time came

bells rang
bones fitted

all the above orders served with french fries

each new leaf on the tree
leads to the world I see

THE LAST TIME I LOOKED

yesterdays

hello, I want to phone yesterday
I want to be the one to wake myself up yesterday
only the phone could wake me up yesterday
I thought it were yesterday
but that was yesterday
yes, this is yesterday
why he est turd eh
I should have done the laundry yesterday
I should have known better yesterday
I acquiesce to yesterday
so water yesterday
the succession of failure was the big story in the papers yesterday
the world-eater spat out yesterday
the television set is stuck in yesterday
the world-eaters spat out themselves yesterday
I found this throw yesterday
& hurled the world-eaters straight into yesterday
this piece of food died just yesterday
we missed the garbage again yesterday
brother, can you spare a yesterday?
I seem to have borne beans yesterday
tomorrow is as far as yesterday
that is what I ate yesterday
don't interrupt me with what I said yesterday
this is the promise I made to you yesterday
we only met yesterday
how did the Mets do yesterday?
how do you do yesterday?
we met only yesterday
how are we doing yesterday
only we met yesterday
the question for tomorrow is the answer to yesterday
the mail is devoted to yesterday
fuck yesterday!

there's no future in yesterday
the word for the day before it is pen-yesterday
in mourning for yesterday
on every morning from yesterday
families are familiar with yesterday
words have a way with yesterday
you can't reason with yesterday
who will pay for yesterday?
there's no such thing as yesterday
everything leads to yesterday
laughter invented yesterday
there is only one yesterday
so much for yesterday

todays

It was days later before I came to a stop. I blew my nose & threw the wet ball of toiletpaper at the tv screen. It flickered just before it bounced off the look of a man who decided not to. I went & sat in the guest chair facing the windows & watched the evening sky for awhile. I just can't keep up with her anymore. Her beauty is in her motion. She moves away from me, toward darkness. There are no buzzards here but there are streetlights. I'm impossibly strong. I can't move. It's always day.

The other day I dressed up for a change for my stroll through the financial district to the post office. I looked like an easy million. Someone recognized me & asked what the matter was. I told him what the spirit is.

The law of the physics states that the second day of coffee is heavier than the first. What was that old saw about typing out the reader's eyes at the moment between hitting the keys & hearing the sound so the word can come first as well as finally? 'Help Help Help!' the peacock cries.

I weigh three or four times as much as she does & I'm thirty-seven years older than her, but we've found a way to wrestle. The opponents lie on their backs with their legs up facing each other, & when the four soles are touching: push! The skill is in catching the other's legs before they lock at the knees. The loser gets doubled up in an instant. The winner gets an instant that lasts a whole moment. 'Laughing & crying at the same time makes rainbows,' she says. In Managua today the people are rising like flies. I've had a beer bottle & a creampuff thrown at me on the street this month by young guys who've taken one look & realized they missed. The kid is learning fast. At me. I'm learning to temper my control, to fight forward not back. There won't be time to say it so I'll write it now – if you can find a way to make it fair, you can win it. Quick – what do you think it means?

Todays Highlights: my share of the nation's phony bill, kids in the toy store boosting their expectations, the preserved bread store, beyond cheese, the Martians just knocked over a gas station not realizing that road maps are free on the really late show, the liver & onion that broke the kitchen's camera, sXmas, earitate, ridiculust, to have great poets there must be great audiences too according to Walt Whitman of Detroit Michigan postmark fame, gales of romance can blow up from the flimsiest of weather reports, a beach to July around on, NYC got to me but I didn't get to NYC, they give him gold injections for his arthritis & he says that's all they have left, veiled advice, old dog don't jump at old meat, I wrote rain/rain wins/rain wrote me/I lost, heaven & how it got there, anaesthetic, psycho-degradable, th!ought, the musicians had it so together before they started to play that the music was just taking it apart.

tomorrows

it seems like tomorrow
kiss tomorrow like a good boy
tomorrow I'll be myself again
tomorrow always comes
tomorrow I get up & have a cigarette & a coffee
to & more & a row of tomorrows, less today
never put off tomorrow
I'll write some of this tomorrow
tomorrow is a legend before its time
tomorrow never goes
tomorrow will just have to wait for today
you know where you can put tomorrow
you know where tomorrow can put you
the word for the day after tomorrow is tunnelday

tomorrow is a school day
any day now is expected tomorrow
tomorrow is a word
today takes tomorrow on
tomorrow takes today off
tomorrow the universe will be one size bigger
tomorrow the government of canada changes assholes
tomorrow may runs out of fridays
by the time we wake up we'll have forgotten tomorrow
tomorrow's child is already hungry
demain/off hand/*au fin*

LADY MAY

I lay along you
love comes over me

what I must do
becomes you

*

walk in & string out
loosen Vancouver & tighten Toronto
wake the gulls & wake the day
fly to Montreal & see if I'm not there
it will be you without me & it will be meat without you
beds are slept & promises kept
you stood & I'm still
the deeper the water & the greater the bouyancy
a shallow paradox & a profound fallacy
I squeezed the mirror & got toothpaste on my hair
I bought this shirt 13 short sleeve summers ago & slow fade
the only thing left is the page & the buttonhole
combing of teeth & breath of spider
out of the crow & into the blink

*

lady
may
melt
me

I fill
a lake
the shape
the shape of
Lady May

lady
may I
make a
river

BEACHED

and through

close the book
it's not night anymore

a fine blue dust
the dawn gets into everything from here

the butter in my moustache
the work in my sleep

I wake with a start
it's not me anymore

it's June
I'm one

it'll have to tell itself
I'm through

I'm to
I'm you

flash tray

there goes a dirty old aeroplane
low over my bare head

bugs hover in front of my eyes
schools of thought swim beneath my face

the tide is higher than the gulls
the sand is warmer than the air

what is that big yellow thing in the sky called
anyway?

I'll say!
'Hey, Anyway, what should I say?

'Here's to you!
'Keep it up!'

well waddaya know
you were here a minute ago

run sheep run

look
the light

the map scratched in the dirt
where does it hurt

a sun
a set

alive
again today

quick
sound

how do you do
how does you do

mountain dry
silhouette west

a hand of writing

kick up some dust to see
the sun find it

I can't look
I'm listening

5 clouds
well, 6

7
'nice day'

'yeah, well I hope the sun comes back'
'maybe tomorrow'

I'm drying my ears
the french have a horn for it

'too bad about the moon'
'it won't get far'

we won't run out of salt

the world is at large
as your hand on my shoulder

the sun won't settle
for less than us

'you're shivering'
'it's the next wave'

'hi there
'tide

'me too!
'as your hand on my foot!'

beach spanish
wreck banks

with my clothes off
I can tell where everything is

absence

what have I got?
enough to last until tomorrow
if I skip today

the high thin cloud
the pressure of last night
I saw you coming

my knee takes wing
it's only a fly
everyone leaves here looking good

I write
you read
ok?

I've been here all afternoon
I've got nothing better to be

      yellowjackets can fly circles around us

    me?
    that was last month

    I don't have to stay here
    we do

    you love the weather
    that's not why you're here

    they are the people who lived here
    they trust us

    say that one can talk
    hear that one can listen

the sun
& there's only one

buys low in september
sells high in July

the feel

I saw a little
that felt bad

I saw a lot
that felt good

I saw everything
that felt right

I saw nothing
that felt wrong

I felt you
that was a lot

I felt myself
that was a little

everything saw everything
nothing was nothing

THE HUNT

the last thing I dreamed
was a couple of telephone numbers

I woke up & it was monday
& a child was calling my name

I put on a pant or 2 & opened the door & let everyone in
or out

I stirred my wrinkles into a cup
of hot brazilian sweat

a bottle flew out of the hotel on the corner
& missed everyone

I grossed $7.80 a day last year
& it was worth every page of it

you're in the way
I yelled at canada today & spat on it & missed

*

well I'm caught up with the fucking newspapers
& I'd rather do my own writing
I mean fucking
come come
you know what I mean
until I get here I can be a mean daddy

a man & a woman standing on the parking lot 20' apart
it's when she moves toward him we see he won't look at her
he steps away but there's a lot of lot
still/to go

to see
to day

for years I tried to spread the honey on the peanut butter
then I learned to cut the slice off the loaf after all that

*

how will it end?
the canadian friend hears about witchcraft on runnymede
& considers tricking britain into committing world war iii
some summer
(the movie *the american friend* is about tricking germany into ww ii)
typing out the century
iii/rd time lucky
so wear your genes at all times
may the clouds protect you from sunspots
may all your little puns be intentional
may poetry be the investigation of history
ending in sculpture
make no mistake
you end me

*

was diefenbaker canadian
is the smilin' buddha buddhist?

dief ends
a prairie lawyer

dief the chief
a good poem

follow john ...
& all the king's horses & all the king's men ...

he ran about the same age as hitler
but more like wc fields than charlie chaplin

unbelievable failure
politics as negative myth

he spoke up
but he talked down

*

flop flop flop
under the clean blue summer sky
the dirty purple tv
with the sound off at last
re-running dief's dire eyes before my very livid life
the voice locked in the box
I'll think to that
of the time that he was typecast as the prime minister
the perineum itself
& I was the propsman
the toenail
walking past the tv studio with a revolver in my hand
& there he stood
in all his pristine arrogance

*

I had thought in the world
as I kept on going like the sand in my runners
to stop
& point that empty pistol at him with both my hands
& let that be the poem
it'd take a life to write

load the words
take a bead on the deathly silence the wealth of this country buys
free the speech
impeach any joe clerk who dares not to be who we are

dief was a brave one-shot hunter
but he didn't have the peripheral vision to be a great prey
so when I turn him off for the last time & the world rushes in
he's nothing left to say

UGLY TITLE

arguments for heckling the poet

a little improvisation never hurt any reading
it's a chance for the audience to laugh
this is not a classroom
poets want to know as soon as they're not talking to everyone
heckle poetry if it's just another thing to heckle
don't be afraid to kill the fatted silence for the prodigal poem
the heckler knows the tune/the poet knows the words
being a poet is heckling the common censor
poets should be more wary of docile audiences than of hecklers
the heckler will lose so poetry can win
help when the heckler can't hear himself shut up
you may forget the poetry but you may remember the heckler

body canadian

I want the music on but I can't write
with her singing about the way I look tonight

I saw your shawl on the sidewalk this afternoon
it looked lost

'I don't want anything flat, that's why I came to BC'
you said to get a rise out of me

the wine went to my headache
the salmon took me up to Granville to get the premature edition of the
    morning paper (get it? I mean, it went on strike only 8 months ago)

the salmon hasn't finished with us
me & my bicycle

yeah
but Reggie Jackson has a manager

she's a buoy
or is that me?

genetics

'Farah Fawcett, Farah Fawcett
'dormez-vous, dormez-vous ...?'

a growl a day
keeps the poet away

an awfully high proportion of the population is dressed to kill
as in, 'Oh – my names are killing me!'

don't turn on the recorder, I'm still talking
CURB YOUR GOD

step on a turd
& break your word

if time is a fly
history is a roach

& just think, thought I
that castle was once sand

smiles & smiles

Reach out & grab it any time you want. (she said to me)

He wants me to tell him what poems I'll read to his students in 9
    months. (I don't know/that's why I quit university 279 months ago)

A tourist staring at Water St. today said, 'Are those supposed to be cobblestones?' (even a bicycle riding over the interlocking brickwork rattles the bricks which were supposed to fit as tightly together as votes)

The Writers Union has raised its dues & writers are resigning. (if their writing is that responsive, they're welcome to join me)

Everything I do in the face of sleep – open all the windows for awhile to blow out the smoke, take a piss, wash & brush, put the dying food in the fridge, reveal the bed, empty my pockets, close the windows to suck in the silence, draw the curtains, position the blinds, close the gate, wind the watch, undress the sight, douse the light – I do well. (but when the phone wakes me in the morning I sound like I'm talking into an asshole)

This'll be short – Skylab is falling & I don't want to be caught writing. (I'm not sitting on a wet bench/I was here before it started raining)

I quickly lose interest in vanilla. (I roll a cigarette without looking)

in fact

the west
of all possible
driving around
one to a chair
are going here
were gonna go there

the rest of the world
for all we know
is standing around
with no place to go

we're not so fast
they're not so slow

best before

When summer ended I was half an hour late for fall this year & I almost ran out of fuel. I know where I lost the half hour (actually I gave it away) it was at the reading. I was reading some of this stuff I write right here all by myself overhearing you & I was reading it to a dozen 100 people, each of them getting to take home 15 seconds (me too, I keep mine pinned up over the light table, like a pin frames the picture it is framed by with its sharp point – but there's no picture, only a pin, & there really isn't a pin there, there are lots of pins there, & each is a time frame ...) so I dooby dooby do believe I pushed 30 minutes into focus, or whatever what we remember is. History. My 15 secs is when I took the cup of coffee, some still in it, although I didn't realize that until I started to throw the cup back over my shoulder, not letting go of it & pretending that it had been full but I hadn't spilled a drop, when in fact I had splashed the dregs over the band's equimpent or whatever it was behind me, or maybe nothing was spilled, I didn't look in the cup to see, I took the cup & made the motion needed to empty it of content; beginning the reading. 30 mins. I was sure my watch was wrong. It's not my watch. I'd rather be writing about the moon Robert saw last night just before it was eclipsed, looking like an orange ball, a really round one, up in the sky – or about the sharp noises in the air tonight. It must be the typewriter. At least I got the dishes done. The fuel I'm almost always almost running out of is the silence that pushes each word apart from the next. It takes a lot of silence to half an hour. A lot of air to strain the rain. While I watched the rain let up, the world slipped up & I caught up. To the time. & time again. Time

– 30 –

lullaby

finish off the coffee
what's the use of waking up early?
no-one wants me before tomorrow

I've lived 271 days this year
pulled snogs out of some of them
planted spemos in all of them

I'm drunk
can't keep my eyes open
or mouth shut

well, brush my teeth shoes hair
squeeze out the rain night beer

well, slip my finger into a hot book
squeeze 'til my feet walk out

go be who's still singing

presence

you discover the music as you first play it out loud & your playing
    will express your response to that discovery.

this is what we do doing what we do

musicians have always played this way – the instruments change,
    to protect the innocence of the future, to protect it from writing

this is what we do doing what we know

the idea is to start from where you left off last time

this is what we do knowing what we know

when music is scored, the score becomes the place & the performance
    of it becomes each time – when music is improvised, the
    performance becomes the place & time can take care of itself

this is what we know knowing what we know

you know that even if no-one were here, this is the sound of this place

this is what we know knowing what we do

the idea is to breathe

this is what we know doing what we do

writual

'Write it down before you forget it,'
I said to D. M., catching up to him.

He muttered something about memory
I'll never forget.

'How you doing anyway,' he said
'Doing,' I should have replied. '& you.'

'Don't ask, he said going into the copshop,'
he said, going into the copshop.

'On the way,'
say I.

or

Nth
America

man

butt yourself out on the door
eat the street

be patient
piss
& listen

lift the toilet seat down

where you stopped & stood
a woman will sit
& start

follow out
lead home

it's hard
this is a fiery year for false premises
try again tomorrow

snow on the mountains

this is a lineup
bank

bank
sigh

silence
like deep

deposits
of bicycles

hard cash
mine ink

mining
time for what I was gonna do anyway

only
slower

bon voyage

you saved up & I saved down

'What's that under your coat?'
'That's my hide.'

as for the roof
I'll fix the sky

when it's stopped raining
you can come back & get your umbrella

I'll fix the light
when it's not night

thank you for letting me say
'What else can I say?'

my son & I dance to the music of my daughters & me
you can't get that at the Paris Cafe
which is the only place you can get anything this time of day

there's a living here somewhere

I grew taller than the wall
the wall didn't grow at all

it shrieks to me like an audience
my eyes rise above it

I have seen the world
it is beyond me

a good song is hard to write
a good singer is easy to bore

'suck me / fuck me / make me write bad cheques'

this writing is as dangerous as painting with fibreglass would be to me
    what with all the tobacco it takes to do

those were stoneware jars of pickles being delivered to the
    Chinese social club down the street today 100 years ago

independently poor is to revolution as purely despondent is to civil
    war

wealth has been wasted on us

we won't be needing a transfer

one moment please

is this the past or the future
we're building?

you know what I want?
6 hours sleep tonight

you know what I want?
time to print the pictures I've been taking since I was 9

you know what I want?
nothing I ever thought I wanted

you know what I want?
the mother to answer the child at the movie Sleeping Beauty asking,
    'Why is the witch wicked?'

you know what I want?
you to call me

you know
what I want

tough titty

well scratch my thermostat
I'm gonna love you when I wake up

hear your ears
here are your ears

I'm never gonna hate you
but not tonight

you don't have to pinch my toes
this is not Canadian Literature

'Pointed Sticks suck!'
'Only the best & your

'mother dresses you
'funny too!'

'BC & Québec is the best of Canada!'
'BC & Québec is all of Canada!'

I think I'll spend my money without thinking

good times
can't count

run to the store
buy new runners

short wait
walk home

eyes rest on the brightest sight
cripples got nipples

work in the dark
sir

bad times
can't tell

last call
free for all

just use the floor

you daylight saver
you band from California

your music is strictly from
what's the opposite of hunger?

junk food
your music is

what's the opposite of strict?
district

of the tricked
the fan hanging in the breeze

opposite the music
what's the opposite of opposite?

ignore the nuisance
dance the simple city

use the proper thumb to stab your knife with

I still reach for the brass fuck
but I don't have to trust anyone under 40 any more

I don't want my share of the tourist buck
I'd rather be in debt to the people who live here

so many damp pants & shirts
it hurts

every row behind me is the 7th row
mom & dad were at the opening of this theatre

modern means
what can change

how come a can of milk from BC & one from Alberta & one from
    Ontario each costs 53 cents in Vancouver?
I guess the basic idea is that rich people need money & poor people
    don't

lyric poems & old steam whistles
won't save the Canadian middle class

                    yeah

                    the tree
                    you don't get to cut it up
                    until you've cut it down

                    the shoe
                    & the shoe
                    you've been walking to

                    the sunset
                    you can always learn something from

                    the dream
                    pat the cat
                    past recall

                    the work
                    you want it all?
                    you got it

LEAPY EAR

monday 1979 / tuesday 1980

it's new eras forever so far
but don't count your 80s 'til they're hatched

80 what?

I ate early
nothing lately

the 70s don't count
don't count on the 90s

the 70s & I split to begin with
so I came alone to the last great party of the decade
disco blaring but I could still hear your comb drop

ash tray, tobacco tin, peanut cup, ol' style
lined up at the watch

word into poem equals worm

80 worms

hot line

songs to hum whilst under attack

fun & games
gone with the rain
guns & fame
they're at it again

Cuba is an exploding cigar

they've got
everything
between us

the bird starts
the bird sings
the bird stops
3 things

hunger practice

profit

I don't have busfare by 3 cents
then you appear needing change for the meter
so we trade your quarter for my 2 pair
dimes & pennies

now you're here
give the floor a little ash
warm as toes
& I'm there
give the ash a little floor
cold as nose

imagine
manna
can't you just
taste it

there goes the moon

what happens is
we don't care what happens
is what happens

what happened to us is
we didn't care
what happened to us

whoever casts the first blind eye
buys the next round
no blame

no one hears
or sees
deaf ears

the image of
true love

write firmly

not now
finish everything else first

I left the party because whats-his-name came
& anyway I was falling in something with the ugliest guy in the eye

eyes staring at the page
words following me around the room

scratching my back
cleaning up after me

the angel claws
so lightly that it doesn't tickle

winter diet
summer live it

the kettle won't boil
with no one in it

read all about it

medium extra medium
you can't hate Joke Lurk

extra medium extra
you can't love Disappear Turdo

it's March
it might as well be a year ago

revolution lives in the anger
you bring home from a day's work

throwing money in a wishing well
poisons the water

spread your spring
weather wings

& shit
when you see the whites of their lies

after thought

this is whistling the same song on this block I did
as a kid

caught up to at
in that bird
dead leaf

trying out
anything but
another hat

why it's monsieur et madame Hulot
hello

& they both smoke a pipe

I want vegetable rights said Fred Astaire
crawling about on Ginger Rogers' feet
trickling through the motions like borrowed money

                thumb nail sketch

        I grew you
        I bit you off
        I hold you up
        I say these words to you
        I pick my teeth with you
        I lick bits of almond off you
        I drop you in the ashtray
        & there you are

        one ear clear
        feet up
        one ear shut
        boots on

        don't move
        this is a poem

                        it looks it

                now then
                now

                then
                now then

                now & then

                then

then & now

now
then

then now
then

now
then now

then & now

now
now & then

READING[1]

dear Saturday
let us return
to the scene of the poem

it looks like I'm the writer in the Joint this set[2]
& the musicians are about to begin
so I will try to hear all I can remember

I put its thinking cap on the top of the pen
it makes it feel a little heavier
& calls for a stronger hand

I'd say *stay!* to the New Era & locked it into the dark
while I take a stroll through the resonance of the last Wednesday
    evening in May
jingling my 5 quarters through the ins & outs of saying so

the man in the revised Ankor asks me
after I give it my walk-through
does it feel better?

& I with a laugh of surprise at the right question say
yeah
it does!

it used to be the place to get pissed – I even took a bunch of pictures of
    a night there once – it was the kind of place nobody said no to
    anybody
then they fixed it & I only went there to get pissed-off
it wasn't an anchor anymore – it was adrift – right into receivership

but now Flakey's fountain's on
& the old yellow cedar Habitat bar has a Blue Jay game on around the
    corner at the end
& jazz is coming from a couple of guys suspended on a stage
    suspended on the centre of the sound

the people are starting to behave the way Deluxe (the builders)
    intended – I trust that everyone's getting paid & that the disco stays
    off
someday I'll come back when I feel like getting plastered in
    Casablanca – sell them the old pictures – take some new ones
but tonight I keep moving up Powell Street to the source

finding & losing random relationships in the crawl[3]
but with barely a nod & nary a smile all the better to keep up the
    mystery
of them on their big night out – of me working on my solo

I lobby my way into the Europe beer parlour
it's peopled in fleur-de-lis-child – like so much of no-cover-down
    Gastown street life – I see their nervous memories everywhere
remember the prototype police-riot they started at English Bay – how
    many years ago was that? – were they there when we got here? no,
    that was the Indians & the Spanish – but the French could still get
    here before us – nobody's ever given the Anglais permission to land
    here – so far we're just hovering

somebody winks & makes a toke-sign at me – but no more sitting &
    boozing for me – not after last night's
I WAS AN ALIEN IN THE DRAKE HOTEL edisode of *stud comix*

me digging slobscenely in my pockets for the joint we were sure the 2
    blonde hugies pretending to be sitting alone deserved in life[4]

Zonk pointing at me who is screaming at them confidentially
do you want some dope?
which rhymes with *nope*

the bunch of us – we'd barely arrived when this guy started barking –
    which made me think we just might not be there long so I better do
    my drinking fast – get disinfected before the hassle
it seems we'd taken this guy's buddy's jacket by touching it
the situation just naturally trying to sucker the newcomers into a fight
    – but little did it know that we are poets

& all it takes to convince us he's a bum is David's comment that he
    isn't wearing dangerous shoes
& immediately Zonko begins discussing this comment – leaving
    George to sit there being brutally observant – & me to sit there being
    corrosively reasonable to the guy whose jeans are meanwhile
    getting tighter & tighter
the Drake wasn't my idea – it's a longshoreman's pub & I haven't been
    there in years – I live 2 blocks away & I should have this typed out
    for one more last time by tonight, August 7th – St. Helen's went off
    for the 5th time this afternoon at 4:30, the very moment I'd phoned
    the bookstore to come & take away my library – followed by a
    phonecall from a Toronto magazine enquiring as to whether I had
    any fiction – I consider this poetry, as in truth (implying that fiction
    is lying) so I said no – & drifted through dinner & on to the last night
    of August where I sit typing this out onto stencils for the Faro
    edition – & way on to the last night of November the following year
    I've started at the end of what I wrote anyway these 4 years & I've
    typed my way this far back to the beginning – but first, back, back,
    back to that night in May, with all the poets getting ready for the big
    reading a few days hence – & not a beer strike in sight & not that *we*
    were wearing dangerous shoes

the buddy, later, shows, in his jacket, to say, *forget it*
I spend the next hour explaining to David that I can explain everything
    – except for that time she never gave me a chance to explain why I'd
    called her Forge Tit[5]

a week or 2 later the bartender admits to the guy with the gun at his
   head that he might as well take the 18 grand – he'd begun by trying
   to pretend to the bandits that the armoured car hadn't just
   delivered bags of money – at the Drake the difference between
   fiction & poetry turns out to be worth about 30,000 glasses of beer

squander your pain
stare at the stripper
you are being punished for what eyes can't see

the story wears out
it was too big for you anyway
the stripper is good! Theresa leans foward to say

I tell her that I dreamed of her
& the North Vandals present think I'm saying that I dream of her &
   lean in on me & she leans away
& so can you! I cry[6]

later Zone & me wine down at the New Era
& then it's earlier & he's out the door & I'm up the stairs, stumbling
   through a tip-to-toe sneezing spasm – a coward's dance
I glance at what the tv has to offer as tomorrow – but is the future
   really just more of America?

finally getting to sleep, cradled in the intelligent stupor of almost
   knowing what's wrong
an intense thirst dawns – a continuous all-night fart leax into the
   all-day shits, real shit, made of Tuesday night's red meat
something like this poem, which takes all night Thursday to type for
   the 1st time – so I can read it on Saturday for the Red Queen – then
   let the final major revision tie up the typewriter for 6 weeks of
   blessed silence so it could just plain rain – then 3 weeks of sunshine
   & I'm stereotyped again – & you may not know what that means but
   you know what I mean

on waking Wednesday I did the least, had a shower, went out & made
   some pen-money scouting books; I avoid my desk & my bested
   British Rail vest & my worsted sardine-bone jacket, sport
I have dinner by the panful alone with the paper radio
not counting the flies[7]

not counting the misunderstandings
we live together
whatever we call it

Canada
I'd vote NO
DON'T GO

Québec –
but I've loved her
so I know how far apart we are[8]

BUT YES
be free but be
careful

no-one's
supposed
to win

inca
nada
kla-how-ya referendum

so, wit out, taking my handwriting from my pockets, I slipped through
    the Europe
& across Maple Tree (not really) Square for a peek at the stand-up
    comic in Punchlines
giving his crowd its heart's desire

there's no-one I know one at a time in the Columbia so I choose the
    Classical Joint coffeehome to arrive at
& discover through the bebop that I don't have any reading – I thought
    I had Writing mag in the bag – & the music is so old – & I don't want
    to go to the reading & interpret last year's writing – last year I wrote
    as much as possible – & this year I wanted to write only as much as
    is impossible – or was that next year – but I can't just sit here
    imagining someone is singing
I know what I'll do – I'll write this instead!

each syllable a page
read it & it dissolves

turn it & it's solid again

give the band a buck
have a coffee
watch the people smoke[9]

stay for a refill
it's not a matter of getting everything into the poem – it's getting
    everything out to see if it's matter – out where you can hear what
    the very thought of you is made of
this is not made out of what happened – this is what we can make out
    of what is happening

I'm now up to what I had in mind when I started this poem
it's what I've been trying to write from notes I made one evening I
    stopped at Trafalgar Beach to rest from all that recycling going on in
    Kitsilano
I left version after version of it covering my desk when I came out for
    this walk tonight

words to nobody[10]
I should have given them to the lovers on the beach when I 1st wrote
    them – but I tried to bring the words home instead
where they had nobody to say it to

nothing came along
everything came alone
you struggle now with yourself then[11]

the more you need love
the more you hate necessity
the more what's actually happening becomes an interruption & the
    worse your cooking gets[12]

by this time it's late July
trying to wring out the laundry without bursting the blister
trying to wait another couple of weeks before we discover why our
    heads are so itchy

there's a fresh newspaper every 12 hours
WHY ARE YOU DOING THIS TO ME the headlines cry

YOU ARE MY NIGHTMARE/YOU ARE MY DAYDREAM I reply
one moment please
one lifetime thanks
remind me to go through this & sow some wild footnotes[13]

after I finished the laundry (including a page about The Tin Drum
  movie which later got thrown out at 3rd) & dinner – & after riding a
  few miles south to deliver the mail to the far-flung empire of the
  New Era – I got home in time for the national tv coverage of St.
  Helens' 4th eruption, which happened today – CTV only had stock
  footage of the 1st eruption (May 18) – CBC had the NBC tape from
  Portland – but the local coverage will be better & BCTV will have the
  KING Seattle coverage, if they don't have their own yet
St. Peter also had heart attacks today
say something nice says someone nice

did you notice how lately women are getting to be nasty – Gracie,
  Gandhi, Thatcher, Sauvé – when necessary to tear down their half
  of the sky
the temperature in Seattle will be 10° lower tomorrow – the fallout
  pattern has spread ENE (from Omak to Wenatchee wide) & is
  approaching the Canadian Okanagan (where it actually got to was
  the Kootenays) – which local CBC & of course Seattle tv know about
  but BCTV doesn't – & BCTV won't have its own tape until tomorrow –
  but it did have on a good shot of the cloud over Yakima – I was in
  Toronto & Buffalo while 3 Mile Island was seething last year & along
  with everyone else I've become quite interested in where the winds
  do blow
well waddaya know – according to the news I'll be eligible for teeth
  next year

hahahaha ha I'm writing faster than you're reading – is something
  bothering you? – wow, Steve Allen, those were the days – I always
  get you mixed up now with Steve Martin
a man without money is like a beach without broken glass
not Dean Martin? – oh yeah, him – & Martin Bartlett too

meanwhile, I can't drink Similkameen Superior BC wine anymore –
  they've somehow worsened it – not that that took too much doing –
  or maybe I'm better
the bottle's empty – that's really what's wrong with it

coffee washes the fast out of my system – if I stop drinking it I get big
fast pimples & a fast back & coincidences – I'd stop eating fatty
foods if I had the teeth to chew grain well– I'd stop eating sugar to
save what teeth I have left if I hadn't quit smoking tobacco this year
to save what breath I have left for poetry[14]

the faces – my sunburn – the pigeon beating up against the window –
the dream last night where you take off your mask
I didn't do that to you – unless there was something I was supposed to
be doing & wasn't – speak up – let me know – I'll be a haircut – I'll
be east – I'll be a deep breath & let the illusion tell me its tale & then
blow it back into its bottle – I'll be new tires on the bicycle, it's
running on my cords now – I'll be a washboard for the tub & a brush
to do denim with – I've already been the sewing – now if the body
will keep on working the way it has these 1st 44 years for the 2nd 44,
then this poem is my half-way mark – I'll catch you next rime
next week begins tomorrow – I have 1 young lady on my mind – she's
7 – & I'm in my 7th 7 – one of her favourite words she made up is
snotril – I call Hondas *bumpercars* – which she thinks is very
marshmallow kung fu

the poem from Trafalgar Beach
or all I can't forget
whichever comes at last –

there were 3 smiles
new moon, old beach
& mine at seeing sundogs

slugs of spectrum flanking the sun, left & right
sure, they're 2 dogs going down with the winter sun on the prairies
true north cold & clear – light-bending ice in thin air

but here the air lies thick & the volcano blew a cubic km of mountain
through it just last Sunday
so those are not just sun dogs
they are sun bitches

& that's us – me, the lovers I'm pointing at the sky to &
the new moon
which everything is underneath & over a little from

including the world[15]

meanwhile, at the Joint, I paid for the coffee refill with the 50 cent piece
    I got in my change at the Army & Navy when I bought a jar of Polish
    dills

now, there's the original notes I made at the beach – & then the 17
    handwritten pages I made in one go at the J – & the original
    typescript which I read at Robson Square Theatre that weekend – &
    it got broadcast on Co-op Radio (102.7 fm) a couple times – & then I
    typed it out again & then I found the 17 footnotes, one for each of the
    original hand-written pages – & then I typed it all out again – &
    made a few photo-clones which I gave away – & then the stencils,
    from which I mimeo'd a flat 50 copies for Farrago (a good buy at 3 or
    4 bucks, like a record only you don't need machinery, just sit down
    with a friend & read back & forth, eh) – & then, just out of sight over
    here on the other side of the typesetter from you, now

so rip rip rip into little bits & into the bag go all available previous
    paper versions – it's like painting a picture or making a movie, all
    you can see is the final layer, or edit, but the lower layers, the
    rougher cuts, do add to the glow, the flow – & somewhere there's a
    videotape of me saying so – but there's something about a
    photograph which doesn't change & there's something about a
    poem which does

there are hundreds of millions of us on the continent dressed as
    ourselves
selling out, buying in
just trying to use up the world before it's all gone

gee, if Peter Sellers can die, so can I
I heard how he & Sophia Loren sat at opposite ends of the front row in
    the theatre, Sellers under the gigantic cinemascope image of himself
    & Loren under the one of herself, watching love rushes of The
    Millionairess
he was one of the great Swiss comedians

I didn't find out until last night that Eliza returns to Henry at the end
    of My Fair Lady, which is not the way GBS lived it
when they make this poem into a musical comedy they'll discover it's
    not the ending that's inevitable, it's the beginning
no-one was as early as I was or is as young as you are[16]

in a couple of days the dust falls as far north as the Peace River & as far
    east as Saskatchewan
some men go 10 years without crying, & when they do cry it's only
    because they feel utterly helpless
each elephant picked up one of the scattered bones or tusks of the
    dead elephants & carried it a few hundred yards & put it back down

Margaret told me about sitting in the New York Deli in Boulder
    Colorado
where they make Mork & Mindy
& seeing William Burroughs stroll by outside

Vancouver BC boy –
baseball mitt, hockey stick, tennis ball
whitecap

odear, the girl at the next table is yawning
this pen isn't fast enough – I'm mired in my quicksandles – walking
    me around & around
the fastest revolving doors in town are in the Marine Building[17]

it took us many months to read Watership Down, the bunny epic, to
    sleep, me & the kid – & we finished it this week
we've seen the animated film version twice
& she realizes what a movie does not do

just down the beach the young Native Indian was performing a
    ceremony
dancing into the water with the sun
or was it the tide getting higher

with me sitting there wondering how to say that the trail of dancing
    light on the water comes straight to anyone who sees it there
bobbing for sunbeams
until they're all gone

FOOTNOTES

1 when you're reading it
   I'm writing it

   when I'm reading it
   you're writing it

2 Like that time a few years ago I wrote *Wholes* there: 'while Gavin's playing ornithology, lovers are loving it, the whole place awakens, I can't write until the guitar solo, here they come again, old Mr. Sax you made a wonderful horn, more, more than wings & engines, it makes us people birds, a shepherd's lament, there will never be another you, undo's my froze joints, last set, just in time, bebop needles sit me up in the light window inside the night, street & narrow, no-one's missing, horn's sweet straight lines to lung honey, tenor sticks tones through gut to wipe loose whole winters of low back muscles, guitar tells me what to say of all people, drums strengthen heart, bass takes big steps out of us all, every through day, do what you do I'm tellin' you, don't take no negative pisces for an answer, gods know, after music passes we become whatever it was we were, Glenn Gould hangs out in Calgary bars, one by one we leave, Good night, good Night, no booze left in us, smiles are miles closer, laughter opens maple tobacco smoke holes in the candle light, this is the writing union I make it to, me & thee over & divided by paper, glances from floor level table people talking to each other, watch chess, an i for an i, say a few Hail Marys for Bob Marley's health, I seem ok up there drawing or/on something, smile forward, sorry I couldn't give you a better game, I'll come back in a couple of years, & the winner has to leave the board, is that significant, Andreas has a way to twine securely the whole day with his understandings in a chat by the door, the floor will get swept, the music will not run silently, may butterflys kiss your teeth with wings, may what happens to us all leave this music free, it's stalking us, to us, let us play, away, the layers & layers, of day, tonight.'

3 Chinese ladies stroll
   as a matter
   hand in hand together
   of course

4 'stuck up'
  is girl for
  'woman'

5 hello young mother wherever you are

  if we're not laughing in 10 minutes we're fighting

  cut bananas with a sharp knife

  buy ginger on a hot day

6 my back feels
  my hair long
  for this world

7 a line of cells all lined up in a line
  of poetry 3.5 billion years long

  that's about 1 year alone here for each one of us
  or three-quarters of the time it's taken for the world to get this far

8 you & me came before & after but not at the same time as we

9   One summer morning when I was a smoker, I waited until everyone had left, then I
     got up, had a coffee, then I woke up, thumbing through Chatelaine, no wonder women, I
     had a Gauloises to freshen the air after by bran new shit, then I woke up, shaved, washed
     the dishes, had a shower, swept the kitchen floor, & went out. The face would have been
     easier to shave after the shower. Then I woke up looking for a Panama hat in the junk
     store, all week it's been closed, across from the old Powell Street Grounds, it's a mission,
     'Prayers received here, free.' I found the hat, half a size too small, 45 cents, I offered him
     my $2 bill & he asked me if I had anything smaller. I did. I said I'd probably take out the
     sweatband, it won't be the last time I do that, & he suggested I try smoothing my hair
     down. Back in the sun I realized I can forget my pale punk polaroid shades, the hat is
     better. I got 55 cents wrath of chicken at 95 cents lb from the girl in the meat market. Bone
     market. Our eyes met. Over at the counter the kid sold me half a doz medium eggs for 51

cents, without looking, moving & counting as if it was me having trouble seeing him. It's
blinding bright & hot out again today. Tenses are shifty. I stay downtown in the summer,
& when everyone's gone to the country, I visit myself. Stroll back to the studio, listen to
David Suzuki play science & Bob Smith play jazz, on the radio, while I throw a flying ant
out the door, make ham & eggs, remember the evangelist's fitting advice & only cut out
half the sweatband, slightly too much, the hat is very comfortable, $11.95, New York,
Knox, a long time ago. I leave it on all day, right now it's the end of my day at my destiny,
I mean desk, tiny under a 150 watt flood, I wrote this at the time you understand, I'm only
telling it now, & the brim cut the glare very nicely. The thing is, the hat is so light, &
shade. I sat at the kitchen table drinking V8 juice & reading a lazy New Yorker article
about Paris. Léaud, the actor, appears, & he's broke too, which is encouraging. The cat
follows me around, limping because she got beat up this week, her hackles got bitten off.
Up front, in my space, I turn the Rio Bumba tape to loud & stare at a chunk of DNA & I
think about subsistence. People with cushy gov't jobs don't think it's an issue. For them,
the issue is what affluence does to them. It drowns them in gravy & they'll never be
criminals again, no matter how subversive they fancy themselves. Down the street the
police are working up Art Crime as the next drug menace. I smoked half the rest of the
hash, it can go on like this, changed from my Molinari shirt to my Gaucher shirt, left my
bag behind & spun out into afternoon. 1st stop Video Inn to borrow a stamp, 2nd stop the
farmer's market to buy an apple, 3rd stop the Old Post Office to mail the letter I wrote this
week, '... watch out for the mountains of love,' it ends. You know by what I was listening
to on the radio that it's Saturday afternoon & the post offices are closed for getting
stamps, & anyways they don't lend stamps. 4th stop Stanley Park. I tell the kid there's no
such word as 'badder' but she says it's funner to say badder. 5th stop, by bus, to the
garden, to water the plants & fry the chicken & pick some beans & carrots & drink some
beer & watch Between Friends & French Connection II on tv, speaking of crime. Speaking
of subsistence, the cat bites my imagination, speaking of poetry. I locked up & walked
here, which is not home, but we don't know it. I remember love. I remember, love. It's 5
a.m. The seagulls. A girl on the street shook her head & clucked at me & my hat. She was
fat. My wind has turned to smoke. I'm not thinking of you, so that you'll appear, & you
do, with your own thought, & everyone's watching for us, & I'm so tired, helpless, trying
so hard to stay alone. I'll cover the windows with flags & blinds & curtains, then I'll wake
up, maybe enough to go to sleep, over there.

0 I'm not holding it for you
   I'm handing it to you

1 *now I say*
   out of light
   out of sight

then I said
all told
I put these lines where even I can find them
like the candle for the blackout was on the windowsill
& more dirt's on the window than between the window & the star
food melting in the fish story
Idaho on the radio
it's only a stare down to altitude zero
cruise sharks on the street
crucial misses
restauranteer patrols the sides in his apron
walks like his wife depended on it
Powell Street power failure
rubbies in the park muttering of loot for everyone
meteor showers in the northeast
trollybus
an aisle of day
rubs by
the hottest night of the year
streetwasher
yellow flasher swirling
beckons
that that that
water works well in the dark
loggers all laid off
forests closed
close forest
hotelrooms all gone silent
protected in a phrase
the writing figures me out all night
the candle a fuse
the world a world
vancouvertigoal
intelligent death
I see the star sees
I think the star thinks
I know the star knows
projected in a face
slower than dark

12 my cooking gets so bad I do the dishes while I'm eating
    my typing gets so bad I do the writing while the correcting fluid is drying
    my lusting gets so bad I do the loving while I'm not looking

13 this guy at the beach came up & asked me for a pencil so he could
        write something on his popsicle stick
    I smoothed some sand so he could write something with his popsicle stick

    but what he really wanted was a popsicle
    & all he left was a footnote

14 each copy of my book you throw away makes the rest even rarer
        & more precious & easier to find

15 a quiet eye
    a fly in the sky
    a clove in a pie

16 we saw the morning glory
    in where
    we see the butterfly

17 don't lose your temper
    use it

FRIENDS & LOVING IN FARO

for Rolling Stone

(rejected)

I live in Vancouver in the southwest corner of Canada. You might have read a poem of mine call *the poem* in R/S, the issue last October with Jimmy Buffett on the cover. The poem followed a Susan Sontag interview, like a rebuttal.

the poem

you are hidden behind the stars
I'm hiding behind the words
we are both in the smoke
I am beside you
let's go over there

the words & the stars are Aphrodite's
the men are planted in the sand
the women are walking out of the water
the radio is on the coffee
somebody is being flippant

look at *that* ant
that's a spider
that's 2 spiders
that's a spider & its shadow
it's calm, just behind the meaning

My books sell in the 100s. It keeps me humble. But my poetry is well enough drawn to be enlarged in public readings to full voice without distortion. Something rings true, & the occasional standing ovation it gets keeps me proud – & makes me think my work must be worth more than the $2264.59 I netted last year. I suppose that my readings are performances, but I do something performers can't, I simply give each syllable, each word, its due weight & let what's being said drive the poem. Spoken poetry finds the music without singing it; as, at the other extreme of music, an instrument will find the words without saying them, if you care. Some people don't, so you can imagine my pleasure at getting an invitation to read at the 6th annual *Farrago* music festival in the town of Faro in the Yukon Territory, Canada's northwest. There's a whole world of folk music lovers who've never heard a poet like me. I went up to Faro a couple of days before the festival & stayed a couple days after. I got back last night. This is the journal of the past week. It's the poem I'll be taking to the next place I go to read.

Tuesday night, September 2, 1980

The book is printed, stamped, collated, stapled & published – *New & Used Poems* – my year's work so far (a set of sonnets called *leapy ear* & a long poem from the summer, *reading*) followed by some old poems, such as:

bicycle

MOUNT
       to project
       to threaten

well pump like mad
get hot
have seasons

OLD

to grow
high   deep

rolling
his eyes
to balance

END
    and
    before   against

REMAINS
        dwells
        the mansion

a long way round
the man the air
sat home in

MYSELF
        the very
        the same

DISMOUNT
                an avalanche
                a valley   a volume

to swallow

8 legal-size sheets mimeo'd both sides, & a cover, 50 copies hand cranked by the author. Everything else in preparation for going is done, too, even getting out of bed one time to put the Vancouver-Whitehorse-Faro plane ticket in the shoulderbag where I won't forget it. I will forget to put my kid's shoes away & to pack such potentially vital items as earphone & RCA-to-phone jacks for the cassette tape-recorder, & a penlight, & someone else's book to read in the northern night, & a few mushrooms for the good fight.

Wednesday morning

I got about ten seconds sleep before the alarm buzzed, half a dream early as usual, but I'm content, I did get the laundry done, I'll be able to come home in a week & make a clean start, & writing this journal is a better move than reading another Swedish mystery, & saving those mushrooms to come home to should make the old typer smoke away as it works up these pencillings. I got up & did my everything, ending by throwing the list away, putting on my black 1955 army boots & getting out the door. My bag full of books drags me the four blocks to the bus stop. 50 cents later I'm at the airport.

Catching a plane really is catching up. Me & the great-white-retail-tycoon hunter beside me – he's after a bear & there's a Greenpeace party up there hunting for the likes of him, no wonder Customs wouldn't let him bring his pistol, & I'm pleased we flew over clouds all the way to Whitehorse because I didn't want him to see any more of Canada than necessary – I wonder what I look like to him, me with long hair snapped back in a ponytail & an inhuman distance, near or far, in my blue eyes; & him looking like a down-size Jim Backus rerun in b&w. I turned him off & read the Province, felt the Polish strikers go back to work, took a deep breath for Terry Fox who has had to stop his one-legged run across the country, raising (as it turns out, 23.5 million) bucks to fight cancer, & his cancer has spread to his lungs. I ate everything they gave me, screeching to a stop at the toothpick. I cleaned up a copy of McTime with my Staedtler 317 fine-tipped black marker. I searched out the window for familiar clouds. 38 years ago I started school in Prince Rupert, 500 miles north of Vancouver, & it's taken all this time to get twice as far north – will there be any left, of whatever it is, that makes almost everyone down south shudder? Canada doesn't have a deep south, it has a deep north. Between the clouds I can see the northern autumn, dark green, bright yellow, deep red, & the blue & white & green of water. The first snow fell today in Dawson, 300 more miles north. There will likely be snow on the ground next May.

From Whitehorse, Canadian Pacific Airlines took their Boeing 727 & shoved it back to Van & I caught the Trans North Turbo Air's next De Haviland STOL Twin Otter to Faro. Me & a few other guys, including the piano tuner & a kid on someone's lap in the co-pilot's seat, sitting very still, all of us. We land neatly on a gravel strip, about 5 hours from the mouth of the Fraser. We are up on a plateau, looking across the Pelly

River Valley to the town on the other side. The lady known as Katy
drives us there, keeping well to the right on the 2-lane gravel road – we
are being passed by 100-ton trucks loaded with containers of lead & zink
concentrate from the Cyprus Anvil mine's daily 10,000 ton production.
The trucks take the concentrate to Whitehorse & trains take it to Skag-
way, Alaska, & ships take it to Japan & Germany, where I suppose it's
processed, manufactured & sold back to us. It's the biggest mine in the
Yukon & Faro, with 1600 people, is the second biggest town. The little bus
drives up to what in Britain would be called 'semi-detached council
houses', new but obviously, if mysteriously, not owned by the inhabi-
tants – only the mining company is the owner here, providing all the
facilities necessary to achieve a stable workhorse, I mean force, whilst
discouraging any permanent attachment to this place. The buildings
face each other, not the wilderness – the wilderness, in fact, burned
down the first beginnings of the town & burned itself down for miles
around, in 1969, on Friday the 13th of June, leaving dead poles standing
above waist-high second growth, where once the spruce & poplar raised
life 20 or 30 or 40 feet above the rich moss & the poor clay. So the forest
doesn't loom & the past doesn't press & the future runs out with the ore –
which, knowing industry, will be as soon as possible. So much for the
obvious. Faro was designed in some city but there are no such cities here.
This is the Yukon. When I get home in a week & describe to my mother
the mysterious, unlocked, open-hearted people I met & looked in the
eye, & my feeling that I'd discovered a resource of honesty & clarity in
myself as well, she simply said, 'Why it must be the way we used to live.'
In town the bus dumps me just as a gigantic toy dumptruck drops a pile
of topsoil beside me. 'The lawn,' it's called, & I'm introduced as, 'The
poet from B.C.'

It's better to make 1000 a week than 1800 because taxes shrink the 1800
    to 900.
When you slide off the road in the truck or fly into the bush off the
    trailbike, put on your helmet.
Everyone pays for the TV dish, to get Home Box Office, San Francisco &
    Atlanta as well as the Canadian Broadcorpsting Castoration.
I've never seen such good record collections – if the museum being
    talked about happens, they'd make a great exhibit, the archaeology
    of entertainment.
Someone moves in with his girlfriend, so I can have his room in a

bunkhouse – I get used to the acrylic dryness – every once in a while the room begins to shudder, it's not just me, the little yellow & black silk flag, THE CITY OF DAWSON Y.T. INCORPORATED JAN. 9, 1902 'IN GOD WE TRUST' is quivering on its little white pole over there on the dresser in the opposite corner from the bed over here – the bedside table is a little refrigerator.

In the cafeteria the roast beef is laced with garlic & I eat more & more of it until I'm walking around town because I can't sit down.

An ordinary drive in the Yukon can be hundreds of miles because that's where the destinations are – it's all linked up together into one big place for the people who live here.

I watched kids playing & dogs playing & began to remember how well I knew wild places once – the ravine in Toronto, the back bush in Rupert, the slag heaps in Sudbury, the bottomless lake in Victoria, the hidden cliffs of Vancouver – up & down – paper is so flat.

On the plane to Faro when the clouds opened I opened my eyes & when the clouds closed I closed my eyes.

I've given away 4 copies of *New & Used Poems*, helped in building the big stage, started discussing the idea of me doing a reading from it – the Canada Council, which is paying my fare here & $150 for my Saturday afternoon workshop reading forbids readings that people have paid to get into, as part of its policy of keeping poets poor & unpopular.

Drink, smoke, stay awake as late as usual – well, that's all right & this is all writing.

Thursday morning

The blanket crackles. There's a long, flat, eery moaning sound outside early in the morning, then the clock-radio pops on, then I sleep in. The people putting on Farrago are doing it on top of their regular work. I wake bleary, climb to the cafeteria – the town is on two benches, above the river & below the hills – but it's too early for lunch so I go back down to the bunkhouse & shift to shitting before breakfast – of breaded veal cutlets & the trimmings, the only thing I could refuse was the soup. I could live on one such meal a day, so I go buy some oranges, apples, gingersnaps & soap to see me through to it.

The main stage at the rec centre is being framed with poles, with the backdrop a mock-up of the front of a log cabin. I find ways to make myself useful, & get in a couple of trips to the hills behind town to harvest some more dead poles. Good guys, good dog, good truck, a bit of trouble with the chainsaw & it's back to the axe; & yes the mine is dirty/so get regular bloodchecks for lead; & yes those birds as big as seagulls are ravens/you should see them split up/a couple decoying the bear while the others grab his grub; & yes those are formations of sandhill cranes migrating/the V's changing shape the way schools of fish shift direction; & yes make a little collar for the roach from a split of paper-match-cover; & yes you take a tour of the mill/you'll find something to write about; & yes there's curling & hockey teams & snowmobiling & cross-country ski-ing; & yes that was the soundcrew you flew up with yesterday; & yes Ross River is a Native Indian town a few miles down the road/but no there aren't many Indians working at the mine & without them Faro is not a typical Yukon town/the Natives up north on the Beaufort Sea oil crews are integrated with the whites/but not in mining; & yes up on that bluff where those guys are dancing around & drinking you get the best view down the valley; & yes the north might well bring out the best in you.

Over to dinner, sirloin steak & easy on the veggies, read the White-horse Star ('Illegitimus Non Carborundum') about a guy who walked into a bar waving a pistol he'd just stolen – the police got him into the police car with no shots fired but he kicked out the windows with his bare feet. Then down to the room to freshen up, change into my sweater, have a neighbourly fourth toke of the day, float back up the hill, check out the centre, slip away to the coffeeshop in the hotel where I sit with a guy – I suppose that people here are friends until proven otherwise. We talk through his dinner, about when you quit smoking the energy it takes to reclaim the energy tobacco used up, & the dancing there is to be done if you've got the lungs for it. The rest of the evening I hang around the rec centre watching the stage get made & the crafts fair getting laid out. I make plans for some reading to English classes in the high school next week, have a beer in the pub downstairs in the hotel, & talk, & get back to the bunkhouse for the sixth hit before a good night's leap.

Friday morning

That moaning again & I saw the husky doing it as I ascended to the upper plateau of the town, stopped & looked back down the cliff at the light-footed high-throated poet in us all calling the sky – which reminds me to start noting down the poems that are coming to mind to read. I don't expect it to be quiet enough for a poem like:

> life magazine
> pictures on the wall
> starved kids
> to make me eat
> the logic of it

I have some mighty noisy ways to say that, that all steel was stolen, that the super-rich are an alien species (Darwin, Marx & Christ oughta work on that one). My last hefty cafeteria blunch before I start eating with the musicians & organizers. Then something crumbly whilst firmly parked in a 4-WD outside the rec centre. I'd wondered where those spices went, they went north with the good-paying jobs. I go into the big gym to find the main stage completed – if I'd hung on until 4:00 a.m. I could have joined the celebration, but I was probably wise to get to bed early, after recording some choice cuts of the chainsaw chorus. Now I have my bookstall to set up in the crafts fair, which is in the boarded-over curling rink, with an art exhibition at one end & a mining company safety show at the other; & pots, sweaters, knife-sharpening, native leatherwork, painted goldpans, loose moose graphics & a hefty etc. in the middle. I'm still giving away copies of *New & Used* & meeting teachers & librarians & shopkeepers, for whom I have arts magazines, book catalogues, video news – useful stuff in a place where most travelling is by post. The video-tape I brought turns out to be in the wrong format for their equipment (which hasn't been used yet, because they have no tapes for it). I brought a bunch of posters which show me in silhouette reading, & say, 'GERRY GILBERT & POETRY,' & I get to work writing the time & place in, 'at the coffeehouse – free – Saturday at 1:00,' & sticking them up all around town. Farrago is underway, the musicians are popping up everywhere, the hotel is crawling with talent. I get my performer's kit, with maps, mining co. blurbs, meal tickets, my badge, last year's Yukon Annual Report, plenty of tourist information & a deck of safety slogan playing cards. The 1978 population figures are 23,306 residents in the Yukon & 364,000 tourists. I check into my room, give a deep breath, & it's on to the opening banquet upstairs at the rec centre in the coffeehouse. I sit with Faro folks I haven't sat with yet & the moments we have/is the music I came for. I know an imported musician or two, from a distance, but I don't have any actual cronies there. This kind of event does have a competitive business aspect to it, everyone very busy being entertainment, one after another or is it one before another. The poets present are of course supposed to stand outside any ambition for a future – oh yeah? I need work too. I wasn't invited here to get on the main stage & do a set in an evening concert, but I'm spreading the word that I'm interested. There is a Yukon poet present, Alyx Jones, young & hardrock. We meet & he comments that the set he'll do on stage tonight is fast & easy stuff for the crowd – shades of ol' Steven Vincent Banal's fiddler's contest come to mind – but when Alyx recites it's tight, clean, tongue-tested work, delivered from memory & intercut with a spontaneous commentary which is part of the poetry. His set is ten or fifteen minutes in five hours of music. The audience of 700 is sprawled on the floor. The musicianship is tops – & half of the performers are from the Yukon. I keep remembering Scott Shearin & his bass flute, Ferron from Vancouver who sings her songs with psychic accuracy, Joe Loutchan's country fiddling that made my feet itch, Kathi Cross tiny & round who put down her baby & picked up the room, Stan Rogers & band whose song 'Barrett's Privateers' is the basic ballad of the decade – you start singing the words & you find the tune. I split my view of the stage between the gym below & the performers' lounge above, looking down over the stage through picture windows with the mixed sound piped into it, like a tv control room. In real life it's the martial arts room, where one learns precisely how far together, or is it how near apart, we are. Some of the musicians get up on stage & belt it out, some try to tune themselves to the audience. Most of the patterns are already well-known, but no-one is treating them as routines, everyone is paying attention. Originality is not the necessity here, care is. I hear room opening for improvisation beyond the plain structures, the simple verse-forms, beyond those limits on content which emasculate our 'popular' music. I hear an opening in the generous but still hopeful sound of the applause & I see it in the hard-won experience of the people I've met here & I trust that the central tradition of our folk music still is to bring us home to where we live together, & not to spin us apart into our private fantasies; & the intensity of this occasion proves to me that love & friendship is what's happening, not the making of money. I realize, too, that if I as a poet get up on that stage it won't be to entertain but to search out & destroy those control systems & habits of language which are attacking our bodies, our body. The same one, ones, sprawled over this hard floor all evening, being strengthened by this good music.

The music protects us, the poetry heals us. Poetry as talk dancing. (As once when I danced with a dancer, dance became walk singing.) I like this sitting here typing, working out the places on the pages, & I liked being in Faro, working for my place. I usually have an idea of what might happen, but insofar as I don't deal in desired-effects in the pursuit of artistic-ambitions, the poem discovers new territory in the imagination, where we can live our karma in truth, not fiction. (I like a good story & a fat cheque as much as anyone, but I'm not addicted to them, I don't worship them, & I can do without them.)

There's the threat of a strike here, a conciliator's coming next week, & the threat keeps community an idea with a shaky future here – but the person who told me that got here when she was twenty a decade ago & her kids were born here – & it's the people like her who are the hope this town has to become a democratic community. It's not for me to say whether the town is well-built enough to be worth it to buy or otherwise take over from the company, & to clean up the mine, get in some co-ops & do what any community can do if it gives itself the time.

Me living in downtown Van I should probably have my blood regularly tested for lead etc. too.

Farrago is studded with imported rent-a-cops in brown keeping booze, gate-crashers & dogs from the door & separating the performers from the audience, sorta functioning as living lucky number programmes, the kind you can't tell us apart without. 'Will the folks whose young husky or malamute is tied up outside please go & quiet him down, he's got half the dogs in town howling!' & a couple of mounties stroll wherever they want to be not particularly appreciated.

You were saying how the trees have to struggle so hard to grow.

You were saying it's hard here for the teens, so many are from someplace else – & in a slip of the tongue you call them 'the audience' & I guess they do watch us perform.

You were saying everyone here has all the facilities they need, cameras, trucks – the Yukon has the highest helicopter population per capita in the world – but they're just toys, that your long-term family goals depend on the stake you're making here.

You were saying that you may be leaving Faro but you won't be
  leaving the north.

The concert ends. I lean up against some halls watching folks – I think
this used to be a folk festival, now it's called a music festival. Splat splat
through half an inch of mud, slip down the cliff again to the room. My
neighbour says he won't be attending until maybe last night. A few stars
punching through up there. Abbie Hoffman gave himself up, I read at
breakfast. I'm the rescuing angel with the two reserve cigarette papers
from the back window in my wallet for the neighbour, I hear his
heartbeat-bass music now instead of the room's characteristic buzz.
That smoke detector doesn't need winding does it? I'm so aggressive –
nobody else put up posters for themselves. 2:30. I always sleep alone.

Saturday morning

I wake gradually from 8:15 on, slice my orange, shower my self, saun-
ter out to the blue – I go out a door here I usually head straight off in a
wrong direction. Wrong is the wrong word, right isn't quite right either,
I like getting lost so I can find myself. In my muddy boots, fresh snow on
the mountains behind the hills, fresh frost on the poplars. Poplar silence.
& in my pocket I find the roach for the road to breakfast. & on the road I
look up & find Al Simmons, the clown from Winnipeg, dressed up in his
refugee-from-a-human-jukebox-costume out parading about, giving a
hoot, worth a wave & a wiggle in greeting. First stop the rec centre where
there's a film festival going & on the main stage a 'Tribute to Tradition'
concert & somewhere else a children's concert & upstairs a 'Philosophy,
Politics & Introspection' workshop & in the curling rink the crafts fair is
bursting open. I stash my bag (very great today with books, tape
recorder & meal tickets) in the office & hop a ride to breakfast in the
Union Hall – which is actually, surprise, also a bar & a cabaret as is the
Legion Hall & maybe the Nursing Station & the cute pink church (they
say it's ecumenical & isn't booze?) for all I know. All I know is I'm hun-
gry for the scrambled & bacon & coffee & the charming speech Ted
Harrison delivers, about creative people being there to wake everyone
up – the image he uses is a fish tank in a Chinese restaurant with a catfish
in it to keep the carp darting about in alarm like birds. Ted is a round

robin of a man, a painter of dream-bright scenes, who lives in Whitehorse. I met Eva Van Loon, poet, who will be sharing the workshop this afternoon with me & Alyx Jones – I spot her poems from over her shoulder & close in on them right away & they are real, lying curled in themselves, like eggs.

Cut to: the workshop, Eva's poems are light & much quieter than mine & Alyx's & than the audience (coffeehouse can't stop) but they get their hearing & I'm pleased our voice includes such open space as hers today. Alyx says he doesn't like workshops much & hasn't brought any texts, so he moves some poems out from memory, him & me keep going fast & loud, amplified into the coffeeshop clatter. I try to get some decent sound from my tape recorder of me reading so I can accompany myself but the audience complains of the noise, so I stick to live, spin through some prayers & some travels around the country, it's not that far to the Okanagan:

> goodness & mercy are following me straight across the lake
>   from Summerland
> the porch screened in a tear in the sky on Naramata
> swimming back on my back my cock my skin
> July 23 1966 Montgomery Clift died of natural causes at 45
> grass & apricots & coffee & water & heather
> the whole afternoon she just wants to make something that's pretty
> day & night irrigation sprinklers
> the lane first left after Ferris over the Middle Bench Road
> apples growing
> let her
> she doesn't understand a word
> From Here To Eternity
> please don't go without leaving

I can see people listening closely, & I keep going for an hour, until Alyx suggests I wind it up, which I do with *reading*, which is the first time I've read it all out loud, which is the time that the surprise in my voice is perfect, which is how come your first reading of it is better than anything I can do now, which is why it's not necessary to rehearse poetry, which is:

> ... to say that the trail of dancing light on the water comes straight
> to anyone who sees it there
> bobbing for sunbeams ...

The poem goes on all summer, which turns out to be a very singular 15 minutes (sans footnotes) – clap clap clap – & I pray back, & relax. In such a loaded-with-performers atmosphere, one does one's #, feels the empty hole with one's tongue, & wanders on to the next stage. I grab a salad & get a custom-made tuna san & make for my tables in the craft fair, where I play some drumming on the tape recorder & catch up on the journal here & chat with people & sell some books – $14 worth so far. The blank video equipment sits there waiting to be lugged back to the library. The librarians are interested in the video series in the new library in the new year in the new wilderness. The Human Jukebox comes on & I take a quick walk around the festival removing my posters from the walls & doors. This writing there's time for in my travels uses the time at home when I'd be busy with my domestic habits & routines. On the road I strip down to me. To do that without leaving home is as easy as quitting smoking. To find the next thing to say is as easy as staying open & waiting for it. So I come back & man my stall. A blind singer comes & buys a copy of *New &* – it takes him right back to Vancouver, it does. He's sorry he couldn't hear more at the reading. I assure him, as I've been assuring the audience one by one as I meet it, that I'll have my moment on the main stage tonight or tomorrow night. & save the margins for me, on the main page. & time to walk down to the room & change into the sweater & lighten my pack by taking out the tape recorder – I hear much better without it, & as for recording what's happening the notebook gets down what I learn from what's happening which can be a happening in its own right & not just more endless idle documentation. Memory, with someone to talk to, is best of all. Dinner tonight is another level down at a picnic site not far up from the river. Steak is being barbecued & the musicians dare to stop singing for long enough to eat it. There are good bones left over for the dogs & the leftover songs that get sung include such silliness as 'Dropkick Me Jesus (Through The Goalposts Of Life)'. I land beside someone so beautiful the backs of my hands begin to ache & rain begins to fall. The scene changes to a mobile home ('... but they took the wheels ...') around the kitchen table. We talk about resemblances, the archetypes we sometimes recognize in each other, looking out at, in to, & after, each other. We talk about how, even in a town as small as Faro, one's responses in public, or on the job, become automatic – we create the strangers in each other, avoiding disappointment like the plague, & in so doing we infect the community with the disease of alienation & make our own lives private. We talk about building our lives again with love & building the community again with politics. We talk about all this, but we can't quite say it all – we hear it, in the music, like an instinct.

& the poetry, if it ever comes, will give us the meanings to be here. Poetry=Tactics. Music=Strategy. We don't stop to figure that one out, we high-tail it to the evening concert. The dog tied up outside is howling tonight, not last night. Tonight the sky is empty & the world is teeming – yea team! I clear myself a spot at a table in the performers' lounge & resume my monkish scribbling. Someone is singing 'Great Balls of Fire' & it occurs to me to send all this to Rolling Stone, after I've gotten home & typed for a week. I remember when R/S believed in writing. A willowy blonde is singing 'Johnny I Hardly Knew Ye' (the source of 'When Johnny Comes Marching Home') – she's Janine Dudding, playing the Celtic harp, & the voice, the song, the harp, they make an immediate hit on everyone's headbone & we don't just applaud, we cheer. Apparently in the previous few Farragos the sound of solo balladeers was becoming mournful, so this year there are more groups, & the soloists who are here (& it's soloists who are always going to be the big hits with the audience, when it can let them be perfect) have it made. Then the country begins to swing, with *Fat Chants*, a trio from Edmonton. The trend on stage is for bands to get bigger as musicians irresistibly begin to sit in with each other. A farrago is a mixture, a medley; confused, disordered, irrational; designed to deceive. Ah, life. I hear that there's a Tibetan monastery at Carcross, where it's being perfected. Gerry joins me. We were loading poles together the other day. They spelt his name wrong, with a J, on his badge, & he lives here – I don't & they spell mine right – poetic injustice. Talk hops to the Bay of Fundy, gigantic Atlantic tides, eclipses, ball lightning rolling down the road around the corner over the wharf & into the water. At intermission everyone is allowed in & it turns into a Saturday night country dance, with the Whitehorse band *Goin' South* whippin' up a winter storm. Some of the people here sure are big, I see when they stand up & start stompin' – reminds me of a long ago rock festival at Aldergrove which pulled in 30,000 people from all over B.C., I had this strange experience as I walked closer to the stage, the men were getting bigger & bigger & the guys standing right in front of the speakers had hooves & tails. Tonight I wander back to the room early, there are dances on at the union hall, hotel & the Legion, I hear. It's 2:00 & I'm on the bed & a good thing it is, too, I'm sure, & I close my eyes & wish the grass seeds scattered on the hard ground all around the building good luck.

Sunday morning

I didn't find a crack in the music for any poetry, but I slept dreamily for nine hours, woke, pulled an applejuice out of the fridge, popped a vitamin, dressed & grabbed a Street Machine Magazine for a free trip on the can, wash, brush, tie back my hair today & leave my toque on, in all modesty, & in case of audience there's always my New Era Social Club t-shirt under it all. There's sunshine out & I'm glad to be there too, or to be sitting at the table of books, 'Lots of winter reading in those fat old BC Monthlies,' the literary mag I bring out, $32 worth sold so far & lots of advice offered, smiles shared & free samples given, in all directions, & coffee drunk. By four o'clock it (wake now/shave later) dawns on me that I better start hustling now or forever hold my piece of paper & be quiet. I hang out outside the Farrago office after I see the producer go in & then I slip in after my ally, the arts & crafts co-ordinator, as she is telling me that she has done all she could but there is no room for me in tonight's line-up, & the producer looks up & gives me the same message, '... no, sorry ...' & looks down. I suggest before the concert, I suggest after the concert. I have to squat down so I can see her face, & then stand up before it looks like I'm on my knees, & then walk to the door, & then come back & suggest, '... during intermission, just turn the lights up a little & intro me for those interested....' She has assured me that her only problem is time, that she is not trying to protect her evening's programme. I believe her. I detect in her a solid indifference to me. She can't be bothered to face me. Maybe everything is going so well with the music the rest of the world seems unimportant. It's like that with poetry. But we try to be nice & calm, so she agrees to speak to the director about the intermission. I say thank you & go tell the co-ordinator the state of affairs, but she still thinks that because the Canada Council has paid my fare I can't read to a paying public – several times I've explained that when I've done my scheduled free gig (yesterday's workshop) I can do what I want with anyone who wants to do it with me. The confusions stem from the CC's assumptions that no-one ever would or should pay to attend a poetry reading & that once the people in a location had seen a poet they wouldn't soon want to see that poet again – I had suggested to the producer before the workshop that she attend it to check out on how well poetry is working this weekend, but I don't think she did – or maybe she did, & they have seen too much of me already, I'm some kind of bore sent here by the feds on a make-work scheme for southern city early muddle age literary losers – it takes some effort to maintain confidence in myself in a situation like this, but it's all in the writing, my confidence – they just never expected that a good professional poet would show up, after they'd waited all year. I apologize to the co-ordinator for letting my *ego in italics* show, so lacey 'neath my letraset smile. The adrenalin spurts at the very apprehension of an insult to mine art. She understands & doesn't confuse my pointed little purpose by tel-ling me what actually is going on, if anything is. I haven't had much to do with the folk music scene for twenty years. I remember telling Ian Tyson that he had real presence singing, at an art school party in '58. I remem-ber Odetta's first big concert, which was at the Georgia Auditorium in Van then. I remember the first Dylan songs drifting into sets in Van-couver & Toronto coffeehouses in the early 60's – all against a Lolly Too Dum background (Lolly Too Dum was Ernie Prentice's folk music show on national tv in Canada in the 50's, that I used to work on as propsman) & of course the music in the air from the Depression (my babyhood, mom & dad & me on the road, following the seasons across the country) & then the music that drifted down from the Kootenays, guitars at par-ties, sung by the refugees from McCarthy's America who settled in the mountain valleys of B.C. – I had to escape show business & theatre & uni-versity in order to become a poet – but when I return, there is supposed to be a place for me, & the likes of me. I was an actor on the stage once, then I got tired of other people's lines. I was a hotshot tv studio floor manager once, until I worked with Johnny Cash one time in '63 & saw that professionalism was not a matter of mirrors, that it was a matter of work, of sustained intensity. Most of the musicians I've known have been on the various waves of rock, jazz & the new musics – but I don't feel I'm horning in on the folk scene. & I shall have poetry wherever I go. I grit my pit in anticipation & go back to my room to peek in the mirror. Then I sit in a corner of the coffeehouse writing in my notebook while the lineup for dinner, the last one together for all the performers & festival staff, gets shorter. But there's some dark fatless moose stew left for me too. Vancouver poet bill bissett read here last year. He did a guest set for the big crowd one evening, probably working through some of his high-energy chanting. I hear that the song & dance involved grossed some local folks out, poor old poetry. Alyx liked him – appreciated bill's sensi-tivity. Alyx & I make plans for his visit down to Vancouver in the new year, I'll arrange a reading for him & bill somewhere. After the work-shop, Alyx confided that he liked the poem of mine for my father, *a call* – that particular image of a bee looking at the pictures of flowers. At the right moment I ask the guy with the clipboard if he's the director. No, he's the stage manager – she's the director. No, she hasn't been asked if I can do a set in the fifteen minute intermission. Sure I can if I can keep it down to ten minutes. I should want more than ten minutes during intermission for nothing? Not me. I wonder what I'll read? I'll read the last ten minutes of these notes, but they're illegible until I get home where I will spend longer typing them out than the week it took to write them. The next couple of hours are very pleasant as I plimpton my way around the places I've been invisible all weekend, suddenly one of the performers myself. A chat with a guy who's here on a portage on a Yukon canoe journey – he thought I was from Faro. There's a photographer who's been taking pictures I'd like to see, & we arrange to meet in Vancouver & put some of her pictures together with *Friends & Loving in Faro* – in the meantime I find her a couple of rolls of film from a good ol' boy I know, who'll also have some good shots for these captions to quote. I peel down to the t-shirt. As a matter of fact, there was another New Era Social Club member who published in R/S, Taras Masciuch, ten years ago, a photo of bikes & bikers. Boy am I eager. I follow after the graceful piping, drumming & singing of a South American group, *Sukay*, which means to open up the earth & prepare it for planting. With a tip of the toque to bill & a sigh of that olden John Cage saying, that art is irritation, I'm given the mc's mike stage left, I put my books & papers on the speaker case beside me, & begin quietly to plow a line through South America from Allende's Chile to multi-national mining companies to us tonight. The crowd has thinned a lot, but I see friendly faces & the shadows in the windows of the performers' lounge shifting like crows. I see what's desired – I want it too – but:

first the headlines

1973
Between Mountain & Sea
Canada to follow Chile's lead
rough road for Chile
CAN THE NEW CHILE SURVIVE?
THE DANGEROUS EDGE
The question behind the tension – where to expect the counterattack
CHILE INVITES TRUDEAU
Inflation of Violence
Allende challenged
Carnival Crisis
Allende on the Road
CAN ALLENDE MAKE IT?
THE OCTOBER CRISIS
FACING THE BLOCKADE
Breathing Space

Surprise for Allende
The US Goes to Market
AIR FORCE F-5 FIGHTER BEING
    OFFERED TO LATIN AMERICA
Trouble, Terror & a Takeover
RIGHT-WING REVOLT
PEDESTRIANS FLEE FROM CROSSFIRE
    IN DOWNTOWN SANTIAGO
Allende Hangs On
'If Civil War, So Be It'
Truckers in Revolt
More Civil Than War?
Scenario for Chaos
Revolt ousts Chilean Chief
Allende shattered myth with leftist election win
D-J tumbles in New York
Allende backers backing new junta
Santiago paralysed
Meat pie & wine revolution went sour
Latin American radicals expected to renew violence
Army boss heads new gov't as Chile breaks with Cuba
The Allende tragedy
MR NIXON   CHILE   YOUR   NEW VIETNAM
Chile's new junta rulers cite Allende as bad guy
Mrs. Allende at funeral
CBC reporter freed in Chile
Chile junta begins reversal of socialist institutions
The wages of chaos
Resistance continues in Santiago
Chile coup reaction breaks out in Europe
Independence Day parades abolished by junta head
Food gets priority in Chile
Capital sought for mines
Chilean loan still available
Canada can't change anything in Chile
Empathy for Chile
30 jailed by Chile's junta
'Petty criminal' said to reveal alleged plot
Soviets break with Chile
PRESS RELEASE from the Government of Chile
Commandante Pepe captured in Chile
Burnaby man held by Chilean junta
Chile seals borders to refugees

Chilean arrests mount
Saw mass murders, says freed couple
Ottawa urged to let Chilean refugees in
Soccer match goes ahead
CHILE WILL PAY DEBTS
BOLIVIANS HALT 'PLOT'
CHILEAN POET NERUDA DIES
STADIUM SLAUGHTER DENIED
Junta tracking down Allende aides
Canadians still held
'Rich world' brought down Allende
AFTER THE FALL
The Bloody End of a Marxist Dream
The Military & its Master
Leftist plot 'smashed'
US recognizes Junta in Chile
2 BC men still detained in Chile
Chile abolishes labor organization
Poet's funeral turns into Red demonstration
The Dubcek of Chile
SMOKE OF BATTLE CLEARS IN CHILE
Soldiers burn books in street bonfires
Gravediggers overworked
Chilean authorities relax strict curfew
Opposition to Chilean junta urged
Chile ops out of Pan-Ams
Canada will 'wait & see' on Chile gov't
Failure of Marxism calls for no tears
'You're headed for the cemetary'
ITT OFFICES TARGET OF 2 BOMB ATTACKS
Anti-junta committee formed
UBC teachers ignorant about Chile
Death of a determined man
Bodies jam morgue in Santiago
CHILE AIRLINE OFFICE HIT BY BOMB, 10 HURT
NEW ZEALAND HOLDS BACK
Canada recognizes junta
Schools reopened in Chile as junta freezes wages
Santiago morgue processes 2,800
Lewis hits Chile stance
Chileans facing bleak year
Did CIA money pay the truck drivers, doctors & dentists?
Sedate embassies become 'prisons'
    for people awaiting Chile escape

My voice lost hold & trailed off while I was reading the headlines, but they continue to speak for themselves. Keeping up the change of pace I punked straight into *valentine/79/because I'm mine* (PUCK SEX/fucking your face off ... etc.) & in the following hush I read quietly for awhile, from the footnotes to *reading*, which I didn't get around to yesterday – my latest work, or what's a reading for? I slam-chanted the song *zombie* to ever diminishing applause, & finished with a bit of flaring nostril stench bliss called *she hole he bang*:

> ... I'd make my own rich cuntly stink on the front of my forefinger by rubbing it over my moist asshole, or between my hot toes, &, inserting my thumb in my mouth, I'd rest my finger presst up on the openings to my nose ... then I discovered that other people smell even better than me. They are marvelous to sleep & dream with. Skin don't sleep ... I have to take my false teeth out to suck my thumb now, & to chew the her in her out – tongue gets deeper into the throb than ever ... Roots are underground. Dig over there. That feels good! The wind blowing the fine hairs on my back like it's blowing those trees. Like last night's earthquake made it all right here. There are civilizations we don't know about because they didn't build empires. They just fucked along for thousands & thousands of years. I bet they smelt good ... People are everywhere, furry genitalia buzzing, loaded with memories of the futures they have lived in each other's eyes....

Astonishing, delightful, especially the recipe for what is locally called muff diving. It had been announced twice that I'd only be reading for ten minutes, so, supposing that I had twenty minutes, I read for a thrifty seventeen. Each minute a syllable, press it & it dissolves, let go & it's solid again. Commercials over, lights out, back to sleep. I watch Ferron from close up & the South African singer Tony Bird from as great a distance as possible, Ferron like a letter, Bird like a phonecall. Pumping decibles was hard work & I sat down against the wall for the last hour of Farrago, with a girl from Findhorn, resting, whispering answers to her questions. Questions are the only things that have answers. Farrago finishes later with a drunken champagne bash around a vortex of fiddlers – people who've been here before sneak away to bed, but I get thoroughly poisoned first, dance Irish jigs, buy a record from Stan Rogers for $7, scare somebody at a party in an apartment, I don't remember what happened, just the gesture of someone pushing me off & my realizing that I'm supposed to be alone – I stagger off into the night, with the warning not to stop until I get there, to bed, around the hotel, past the silver storage tanks, down the cliff, through the locked door, & so to sleep. Waking for a drink of applejuice in the night was not a good idea. Thinking is not a good idea. Sleeping works until noon.

Monday afternoon

Nice weather. Hello, I feel sick. Wrecked. Going. Pack my things together, it's moving day – just down the road to a house, to stay a couple days with a family, husband & wife & 5 year old girl & 2 year old boy. I don't want to use people's names, unless they're performers. I find myself with people who know who they are & it's catching. I've arrived & I'm sitting stunned when she brings me a coffee & insists on talking – about my favourite subject, making a living as a poet. 'You're going to let him *stay*? at your place!' someone who'd heard me read said to her. But what's a home without a guest who's tramped in from nowhere & has the latest news he's been saving all his life; from there. 'I arrive in my 20s as some kind of poet, it's the way I work hard, & I discover that the public school system has convinced everyone that poetry should be ignored...it's everyone whom I'm really interested in, it's me too...I wonder if I'll get to any more music festers...a shop steward from the London docks once told me to put a value on my work – is this worth the time? are you learning from what it brings to mind? do you laugh longer or see farther or something? like some more?' I have all these things I'm always saying. In an hour she drew the poison out of me, & my dreadful hangover slow-motioned itself into the past. 'I'm concerned with the way I flow through all this, like writing – it's a kind of realism you can relate to because you're in motion too, like reading. We all have to become masters of the art / of finishing what we start.' I'm in the kids room in the basement, as at home & calm as the toys all around. The kids & I have agreed that they won't jump on my mattress & I won't pee on theirs – I'm in great demand as playmate, which reminds me of the fond farewells I saw between the kids & the baker from Dawson who'd stayed here during Farrago. The brownies didn't sell well this year, so there are freezers full for the winter in Faro. The winter they say is not really worse than on the prairies, but it's longer & darker. You don't get bushed if you get out in it, prepare cross-country skiing trails by skidooing over the routes early in the season, hockey (four teams locally) is out under the northern lights where the lines of force of the earth's magnetic field curve into the magnetic pole ionizing molecules of something-or-other, creating a living image of the planet's magnetosphere (the same thing happens in the antarctic) & you don't chop up a winter's wood ahead of time, you do some chopping every day. It's already snowed this week in Whitehorse. The Yukon government leader has refused to go to the latest constitutional conference (which opened today in Ottawa live on national radio & tv & after listening for five minutes you know that they can't stop arguing, they're not really talking, they're bleating, they aren't listening, they're counting) as I was saying, the Yukon's political leader has refused to go as a mere observer, & Native Indian councils are having a counter-conference because they haven't been invited to take part in building a new constitution either – the Yukon & the North West Territories are colonies of Canada, local decisions are made by absentee landlords in Ottawa, native land claims have not been settled – there is no representation by area as well as by population in the Canadian federal system – so Canada is like a language without a dictionary. Places, resources, are ripped off overnight & no-one notices. The conference is all squabbling over the spoils. It's not the Canadian Revolution. The politicians trying to buy us off with a new Bill of Rights is like getting liars to write the dictionary. You want a new constitution? I'll write you a new constitution – but I gotta be asked – actually, can I call you back, I'm tied up right now, I have to go up to the rec centre & find that record I bought with 20% of my life savings last night. I don't have a record player so I'll tape it & leave it for mine host whose room I used in the bunkhouse. Tacos for dinner. Maybe the union was suckered in to that wildcat last spring, which caused a lawsuit the union lost with a million dollar judgement against it – the conciliator got the company to apologize & the suit was withdrawn, I later hear tell. But it always ends up meaning that the town will continue to think small because of mining company policies & politics, scaring off badly needed tradesmen & services. & then there's the mine's low reputation, it's the kind of place that when you apply for another job somewhere it doesn't matter that you were fired in Faro. I hear something about Farrago costing $60,000, which is guaranteed by the company. I'm saddened that the union doesn't do the company one better, somehow – it's ironic that the mining company hires the heirs of Guthrie & Seeger & Joe Hall to keep the workers kept. After dinner we watch a little of the General Patton bio on tv, then I go for a walk down to the Pelly River, wondering whether, to turn a phrase right-side-up, there's a warrior in the heart of this poet. Way down to the bottom of the valley. Ah, the grasses all in seed, again this year. Patches of mushroom, some little fists just bursting through punched-out ground, some drowned in what looks to me like black ink, now dry – shaggy manes, I learn later, the young ones delicious & peppery raw. I'm sitting at someone's cold campfire at dusk now, watching the green across the river get blacker & the yellowed leaves go golden, feeling the cold breeze in my hands. Lots of sky for the clouds to wheel around in. The sky is the colour of gravel. The riverbed is the colour of sky. Red runway lights on the high plateau across the river. A plane takes off. I'm walking back, between creaking treebones, a gunshot somewhere, sharp note with echo chaser. I climb back up to town. Two dogs out running together pass in the evening – something in their romping is familiar & makes me feel good. The town on its benches, above the river, beneath the hills, with the fresh snow on the mountains behind, I'd like to be on that dirt bike zipping up that cliff. The town was conceived & designed in hermetically sealed offices thousands of miles to the south & millions of dollars in the past – it was manufactured as automatically as possible & shipped here & assembled – it didn't grow here – it works because it has to. Everyone will be up before seven, so I'm the last to go to bed. Animal House on HBO, Trudeau being sarcastic & Bennett of B.C. being bitchy on CBC North, the ass end of CBC South. I write with a pencil with one of those big fat erasers that fits over the other end, in my big notebook which is a sheaf of eight and a half by eleven paper stapled down one side – it's gone all rolled up now, a day & a half left – I'm fast, silent & portable. I'm easy to stop, too.

Tuesday morning

At first, it's still last night, I can't rightly find the toilet so I pee perfect shot in a washtub, then sleep in the dream where the Vancouver scenes have a new angle & I'm in deep as usual but also in charge of the escape, bailing out from a runaway onto the comparatively soft steel tops of cars, the fridge buzzing something typical. 'it's 8:15 already!' I have some bacon & eggs (f-u-n-e-m/s-v-f-m/f-u-n-e-x/s-v-f-x/n-m-n-x/p's) & walk to school with my books. & at last I can hear myself read, quietly & distinctly, with sometimes a sudden fall & a roar you'll hear for years. I read to eighteen year olds then seventeen year olds then sixteen year olds – as usual the younger the kids the looser their imaginations. I had enough copies of *New* to let the first two classes read it while I was reading from it – & to let those who wanted to keep their copies. The last class laughed through such things as *federal infection*, & their bright eyes watched me say, of love:

on the bed
we held
2 hands, apart from us, past our heads on the pillow
us balling so hard down there

joined over us, hands
balanced us like a ball

the grip

from which point we watch
the show

what lies on us
what hangs

*

a pigeon is dead
borne (carried)

the pigeon in one hand
(the weight)

what do you make of it
(catfood) hold me

hold me never let me go
(both hands)

& I was able to give them a poem I wrote at the birth of my elder daughter, who is now their age:

I will write your poems for you
I will not
write your poems for you

(what a wonderful morning

you are
you are what
a wonderful morning you are)

child
when you were born
it was light
out

all was: the doctor's white coat was:
wet
shining with your mother's blood

I saw
you
her, my girl

this girl here
doing it all
to the least
of us

& the morning
opened, yelling
the most ordinary thing in the world

There were 'What does that mean?' questions & 'This is a picture of what meaning means' answers. They had my hand-written journal to go through & they'll all have the opportunity to see this development of it. I left the students with some difficulty & I left them with some difficulties too, & a poem on the blackboard:

w/the

with
stroke
thee

I remember as a student being invisible to my teachers – they never looked. They taught me things. I grew up being very careless with myself & with other people. The students I met in Faro are learning better than that. I met an English teacher in the staffroom who had studied with the great British poet, Basil Bunting, & we talked for a while about the physics of poetry, of how Bunting casts new light with each new syllable of the poem. It wasn't until I left the school that I noticed I was supposed to take my boots off when I entered. Sounds of hammering in the rec centre, Farrago still being dismantled, I feel sorry I haven't been able to help with that work. I walk across the dirt street & around the shopping & services centre to the hotel for lunch in the coffee shop with the arts & crafts co-ordinator & her kids. Maybe I can come back, perhaps later in the winter (nice to talk about, but it doesn't happen). Later that afternoon there's an impromptu slide show & I get to see country life in northern B.C. & hiking to Alaska through the Yukon. The few slides of mine I show need more explanation than they're worth. I forget to comment to the other photographer that one good photo of something beginning to happen deserves some more to see the event develop, even letting the presence of the camera become part of the event, so that more of the image can be seen. I probably didn't tell you what a good photographer I am because I don't have a camera anymore. I probably didn't tell you that because I don't have a camera anymore what a good photographer I am. I probably don't have a camera anymore because I didn't tell you what a good photographer I am. I'd rather watch things like the scab come off the back of my hand yesterday where I nicked myself the first day here jumping over the fence above the bunkhouse cliff & knocking my hand on the electric outlet where you plug in your car's block heater – I was trying to follow a guy who'd just leaped up, on & over, no hands. Worth trying. Now back to the kids' room & take a rest. Then there's time to talk to my hostess about pottery – she has one in the basement, with a cone-eight stonewhere electric kiln. I lived with potters for years, I used to do their odd jobs for them, a great cover, & they eat so well – they've got the dishes to. I knew I'd find a potter, I should have brought my Mayan cup. It's hard to learn to throw pots on the wheel well if you use a plastic, easy-to-work-with clay – you can pull a 'shorter' clay to its limit, with no energy left over & the form of your pots becomes made rather than designed. She has done wonders, just learning from books & a few workshops. The craft of pottery remains in touch with its ancient traditions – it's there to learn to do right. You don't need to try to express yourself because when you do something right, nothing is left hidden. After dinner & dark I take a walk through town. I never know where I am in a place until I've walked it. On the cover of *The Lost Whole*

Moose Catalogue, A Yukon Way of Knowledge, there's a picture of a Yukon vista & over there in it stands a moose – he's not lost & neither am I. I find the office of the local paper, The Raven, which publishes all winter, first issue out in a few days, & I type out a couple of my poems for it. On the way home I slip into the pub for a $1.60 bottle of beer & sit with the girl who runs the shop upstairs, until the new girl is trained, & we listen to a guy's ribald version of *The Shooting of Dan McGrew* – I should have spent more of my time during Farrago in here. She treats me to one of the $3.60 Grand Marnier & coffees she's sipping & we talk about each other. She'll be going back to her place a few miles from Whitehorse, soon, to her eleven big dogs & one big winter. I was going to drop into the shop Wednesday morning to say goodbye, but I didn't have time, Laurie. I like that, about your dogs being used to you, but not to men.

Wednesday morning

I'm called at 10:30, but by the time I'm up the house is empty. The photographer from across the street returns a coffee cup but doesn't come in. There's time to make a cassette of the new Stones album & sit on the back porch with the two year old talking about bugs & time to make some phonecalled farewells. I ask how best to walk to the airport & my hostess picks up one of my two bags & says, 'Let's go!' Down to the river again, this time over the bridge & along the riverbank down a trail pungent with high bush cranberries whose taste fulfills their aroma, like a fine ripe cheese. The ends of the fireweed flowers seem to have exploded, leaving a bit of fluff like smoke there, where I guess the seeds were shot out. You can canoe a long way on the river. Out here it's a good place for kids to grow. We climb up, feeling strong, quickly, to the airport, covering the space, two or three miles, I was looking up through from the river the other evening. We sit for a few minutes in the sunshine on the sand beside the end of the runway. She points out where the new subdivision is going up – the mine is expanding. I shove a fistful of dry grasses in my bag, to put on my desk beside the typewriter while I work on this. I find a dry rabbit turd & pop it into a corner of the bag, a gift for my unsuspecting kid – she loves it, has it enshrined in its own little clear plastic box on a bed of blue foam. Suddenly I've said goodbye & I'm walking toward the small building where everyone is crowded & waiting, so I go back outside & wait. The mountain peak north of Faro is 6763 feet, the airport is 2450 feet. I should get a refund from the airline for the

half way to the sky I've climbed up from the river valley – the plane
doesn't take the dozen of us so much higher.

Farragoing going gone

we follow the valley upriver, green water, soft cliffs

I'm so proud of myself for not fucking around, I must really want to
   return

winter or not, the Yukon feels much more alive than the arctic desert I
   was expecting, or the post-industrial landscape where I lived in
   Cornwall

when finishing off the bag, roll two instead of one, so you can smoke
   one at the bottom & one at the top

landing in Ross River, it looks like a pleasant town, the buildings well-
   spaced, or is it me, anyway it's not big & crowded together like
   everyone's afraid of something; the two giggling girls at the front of
   the plane get off, the pilot in his trim overalls uniform refuels the
   Otter, a few passengers get on, everyone sits very still & I say, 'Ross
   River sure is a quiet town,' & someone says he hopes the pilot's
   credit card is ok at the self-serve, & I say that if you want it done
   right you gotta do it yourself, & maybe it's the hint that something
   could be done wrong, but we all become silent again; we taxi back
   onto the gravel & pull back into the sky, which I watch fly by in the
   lakes

the snowline's at about 6000 feet, now that's half the height of those
   mountains

looking down from this astral angle, seeing the way things want to be,
   of course that's where the lakes are, & the rivers & mountains &
   valleys & people & trees

I didn't want to honour the mine workings in Faro with my presence, I
   wanted to give this time to you & yours

the Yukon

we land at Whitehorse airport, 2300 feet, in a small sprawling city I'll
   visit next time, toolchests & rifle cases in the baggage, I never wore
   my longjohns, I never remember spitting out the gum

I see in the local paper there's a guy walking from Seward Alaska to
   San Diego California who left Whitehorse a few days ago, '...
   walking on to British Columbia just ahead of the winter,' & I
   dedicate a piece of cake & a cup of coffee to him

no, she doesn't want to frisk me with the metal-detector, as I board the
   plane to Van, with the elegant Scandinavian family of tourists,
   complete with its own video camera crew, & I sit in my aisle seat &
   read & write & eat & I close my eyes & feel us descending & the
   ravens turn back into gulls.

ADVENTURES IN THE
HONORARY DIMENSION

deer
the power that issues
like chairs
can sit
apart

slug
the force that admits
like stairs
can set
a trap

*

the page
in the way
in the way in
in the way into the paper

by this poem
create voice
by this painting
create face

the world we see
when we aren't looking
crosses our teeth
dots our eyes

space the memory of touch
time the anticipation of sight

*

i go alone
breeze

barely naked
what with all this hair

more &
or less

forgiving keeps
giving for keeps

there you are
back

flat on the land
open face

toe snail
(cut)

*

find
we can't find
the place we can't find
we can't leave the place we can't find

time rains soup
neural processes interchangeable at eating
graze along with me until a thought bites

the deer bolts
the slug stops

*

the universe
as such
based on a true story
clean enough to eat sashimi off of
grows on us
grows touch on us

*

throw a story as firmly as night
a man in the grass living to learn

paper peppered with anger
cuts a section across pain

pin it up
on a line of fire

it worked
i'm alone

stalk a tale as lightly as day
a woman in the wood learning to live

paint salted with pleasure
fits a window into joy

sew it down
to a dot of water

*

lap dissolve
the iron age
breaks like a shadow
on reflection

i was totally wrong about the wheel
it wouldn't walk
i might as well have been out of town
this ferschluginer week

the ears stopped hearing
the money run out
the tape recorder wouldn't fix
homesick for japan

living beginning
dead end
science & silence
holding my teeth together

everything i wanted to do this winter banned
everything i promised to do this summer
just didn't come up
on any taken day

honest but horny
human but only
been here before
belly full of head

the iron aged more
in the meter to the floor

than it had
in a decade

*

real life's a glad nite's sleep beside yourself
muscles for pillows, words for dreams
real work's the world that built the morning
a copy by the bed for everyone of us
real love's the dance our bones wrap us around
the light of the hand, the sound of the face
real time's the next stretch the neck steps
drink from thought, taste me want to
sleep the work, attention the pay

*

deer starts
slug nuts
bird ends

a field of
all along

sight
light's
shade

find the bird
lose the slug
win the deer

slime shines
wings brush
hooves cut

wow
oh
ow

*

black ready
white already

blue alleys
red eddies

green angel yells
'sky!'

& lands
by eye

*

'to pay or not to pay
what is a question'

tongue curls into a cone
i am what you ask

hair today
ears tomorrow

hands lap ass
you are where i go

land under
stands kin

is
is ice cream

easing in
to season

you spring
i fall

*

looks like a poem
sounds like a dance
feels like a painting

farts like a chainsaw
you can say that again

'neigh!'

short for
simultaneity
in horse

a whole language in one word
language in one
word

not a thought
take a picture

a mouth of dice
a nose of teeth

new whining
leading to
old battles

when everything is said
does the language run out

swish
like the 60s

is it me or is it memory
is it you or is it youth

*

boulders in the road
well
park the bike
hit all the lights later
climb on the blacktop & heave them clear
& here i am
a pore in the palm of the hand that aches for a thorn
the afternoon of a distant present
summer long enough to dry feet
wet neck guessing which window sun will find next breath
& there i am
going back to morning
& doing it again
nobody listening because it's written down
where it lies on the earth
slime twine
all lies
a total find

*

it fits
if it's

a poem can't help
size lies inside eyes

then he left
then she cried

then
cried

make no belief about it
lost at last

for
got

deer like water
slug like flame

*

play works on faces
work plays on hands
behind dances on backs
transparent borders on lines
bed crawls on all floors
silence falls on deft ears
sky runs on clouds
colour fires on desires
live lives on lives
real hinges on springs

*

the story
it's a case of mistaken envelopes

dealt as pretext
for what we were gonna do anyway

let me take you to the ball
let you give me to the world

pretty allusion to
i wish i knew

a tale
told by a summer

full of shaking spears
signifying laughter

angels got
all my hot water

don't thank me
thank you

*

a deer
slug's antlers
tunnels

in line out
out line in

a slug
deer's tongue
a delicacy

YVR BUF YYZ

getting to the airport

my
faint smile

the 7:30 Granville bus from Hastings & Dunlevy
the sun rises with a minute to spare

sleepy people, east-enders, day-breakers, here 40 years
I pull my bag like a brush past the young Japanese guy & the Chinese
   girls & find the seat at the back across from the I LIKE PUS ('is that a
   band?' 'I hope so') graffiti

with private schoolgirls, 2 & 3, white & brown, in green like me, trading
   Stones' lyrics & dreams
one says to one, 'why are you brushing your hair on the bus?'

to one whose eyes' light
touches mine

her
hello

'because I want to'
because I can't stop now

getting to sleep

I don't know anything about greed
but I want what I know

I might have known the scanner'd find the knife built into my –
    how do you say? – bag
did they really mean it when I said I'd throw it away if necessary?

but I never guessed immigration'd want to read my orange
my seed is my soul

does it show?
my seat is my soil

there I grow again
on the $50 bills the Mounties mount their mounts & face into a circle &
    pointing their lances straight ahead charge the centre of the jelly
    donut

whilst out beyond the circle of horse shit, we lie dreaming of a night's
    sleep
images of FDR in the shifting dust of deficits

do settlers still settle? or has credit raised the price of everyone
    out of reach?
I want to help – if I can just get the electric blanket as low as it will go

buffalo lows

Buffalo people live so in Buffalo houses
Buffalo apartment buildings are so empty there aren't any
Buffalo sky got so big by eating all Buffalo mountain
City Of No Illusions
where the deep-fried chicken-wing flies & you've got to read between
     thee yes
where the best is poetry & the rest is tiring
where if you don't avoid all that fast Freud you'll die Jung
home of *Doppelgangers Anonymous* & *The O.D. Hall of Fame*
where *Progress In Progress* grows *Brandname Kids*
& people greet each other on the street with: *'I'm* not Canadian, what's
     my excuse?'
to which the proper response is: be black about it, call yourself a cab,
     now you're a cab
I'm just kidding, it's not true, Buffalo was all made up
the more you hear it, the longer the poem & the shorter the story
think slow & talk fast
knock soft & ring hard
so long, typewriter – it's time for my fingernails to sharpen

          toronto toes

               Mercy
               The Dav
               Yang St.
               Blore St.
               Spadeener
               Addled Egg
               Quing
               & Keen
               Raunch Valley
               Collage St.
               Yorkvile
               Buy St.
               Frum St.
               Wartsylum

so there we were

pausing on red together like Toronto traffic lights
& turning like sox in the wind
& rushing through old age chased by the kids we sped thru childhood
& coffeeshop hopping around Queen & Parliament looking for
    schoolmates from '48
& hitting Homer for being as totally concerned with war as banks with
    money & cops with crime
& as the sidewalk sweeper I left on Powell St. in Van at the end of
    summer angrily shaking the last leaves off the young trees is totally
    concerned with neatness (as opposed to posters)
& me taking my shirt off & coming as a boner to the All Saints' Day
    Night Blues Dance
no – actually I came as Beau del Aire, with The Bo People (Derek,
    Brummel, Clara, Peep, Rain, Jolais, The Big Bozo & all the little
    Diddleys)
mine/still loving thine/eyes
but ah, the breast you once put to my hand has grown longer
m'dear, chérir, dear ma, dear me
& guessing that the one thing you do gotta be able to do in this country
    if you're a poet worth your salt & paper is still be ready to write
    everyone when everyone finally sends in the one request for that
    one last poem, the one called YOU ASKED FOR IT
Ireland & Ireland – Iran & Iran – or just trudging about with all my
    stuff, like a shopping-bag omen, running interference patterns
    through down-torn owntario, looking for new ways to say
    improvisation
poetry sings faster than the music

goodbye

colour our shadows orange
by the smell

the spell grabs us
by our beginnings

& flies us into the sky where we hold on
by the very horizon

& fall apart shuddering
all by ourselves

the land
by the sea

me
by now

thee
by heart

INSTANT LOSS

the wave that can be waved
is not the wave

my dream bases your light on the guy in the laundromat & I giving
each other the wink over the careful way some people fold their
underwear

man is one thing
men are another

in the dream we make friends, you the coasting Indian & me the
  beached white, standing just inside the new era, looking forward to
  the good times, shaking on it

> it didn't start out as today
> but that's the way it ends up

three cops rush up, level their shotguns & with no questions asked
  blow you away

> I'll stop taking sugar
> I'll give away the bowl

the explosion woke me up – this morning I told Murdoch the dream &
  we wondered where it came from

> too cold for flies
> too old for lies

for dinner I sautéed some milked liver with onions, broccoli, green
  peppers & mushrooms for Shawna & me – she went out to her dance
  class & I washed the dishes & sat down with this poem – when John
  Lennon dies

> someday you'll say something
> so clear you'll vanish

John was our main man out there on the off-chance that the best moves
  we can make really do matter – we loved how he made his quarter-
  billion & we hate how it's cost him his half-life

> listening to the news
> without the music

ever the post-modern artist after our own heart, he goes wrapped in
  his red blood & our green tears, the most expensive Xmas present
  we've given history in a long time

> a word here
> a snowball there

for you the war is over, I thought to the cat I took last Friday to be
  killed at the SPCA & as I left the room we turned back to each other
  for a blue-eyed good look through the sweet & sour bye & bye

> prison is continued for those watching on tv
> shogun/midnight express/playing for time

in the next dream a young asian family is confused & troubled – I do
    not know their language – there's a reporter talking to them with a
    tape-recorder & an angle

> bureaucracies & airlines use cm & computers
> to shrink us to fit their plans & planes

I admonish him, 'you know better than to turn them into your story,
    it'll be the end of them – it's better to let them ask us the questions &
    our writing answer to that necessity' – & come to think of it, John
    sang from us not at us

> what you know is prose
> what you don't is poetry

> what you hear is song
> what you don't is music

sometimes all you can do is take a message

> a poem in Alberta, December 1980
> born in the breeze that froze the ink

don't hang around waiting for me – I'll catch up with you later

> leave room in your boots
> for your toes to walk home in

*

they can't want us seeing everything in action they're so much less than
us they make the word gross gross but we just go love each other all the
more easily outsmarting the system again today with a splash of laugh-
ter revolution the deep end of democracy music to remember by every-
one jazz's are you see an iceberg blues is you hear it but what's there is
rock may it never melt you became us singing to each other you john you
waking up everywhere parallel voices meet revolution on the roll the
dance no-one outdances stink softly & carry a big talk we live they die

FILLER

Take a Fresh Clean Piece of Paper

YES IT IS ME, THERE'S WHERE I KNICKED MY THUMB YESTERDAY

YES IT'S GASTOWN, DOGSHITHENGE UNDER A PIGEONFEATHER

YES IT'S LIVER AGAIN TONIGHT INTO THE MOUTHS OF BABES

YES IT TASTES LIKE SHIT MIXED WITH PISS

YES THIS IS AN ORDINARY POEM

YES IT'S ONLY A FEW HAIRS BUT IT'S ALL MINE & I'VE GIVEN UP TYING IT
     BACK THIS YEAR

YES IT'S THE COLD OLD SUN THAT GOT IN THE WAY OF OUR NICE WARM
     CLOUDY DAY

YES THERE IS AN EGG IN WINNIPEG

YES FOR A MOMENT THERE JUST BEFORE XMAS I HAD A FLASH OF
     CONFIDENCE IN OUR VALLEYS & MOUNTAINS, OUR HEAVENS & HELENS

YES A FUNNY THING HAPPENED TO ME ON THE WAY TO XMAS DAY, I WOKE
     UP, TOOK A BATH (CLEAN SOX ESP. BUT SHIRT & JEANS TOO), AN
     EMBARRASSMENT OF MORNING SUNSHINE ON THE WALLS & THE TREE
     WITH ITS LIGHTS ON, ITS GINGERBREAD MEN ALL SOFTIES & FALLING OFF,
     ME TOO AFTER COFFEE & A BITE OF ORANGE THAT MADE ME AS STRONG
     AS 100 MANDARINS IN THE COURTYARD, & WHEN I RETURN 10 HOURS
     LATER TO HOME FREE – ALL THE LIGHTS ARE ON! WOULD I DO THAT?
     NEVER! & THE ELECTRIC CLOCKS ARE 70 MINUTES LATE – WHAT
     HAPPENED?

PERHAPS SOMEONE ELSE LIVES HERE, SKILLFULLY SLIPPING IN & OUT JUST
    BEHIND & AHEAD OF ME, NIBBLING AT MY TIME

YES WHAT MUST HAVE HAPPENED IS THE POWER FAILING BEFORE I LEFT &
    MY NOT NOTICING THAT THE LIGHTS HAD GONE OUT WITHOUT ME

YES WELL CARTER DIDN'T KNOW WHAT HE WAS UP AGAINST SO NOW
    WE'RE UP AGAINST REAGAN

'YES 5 MINUTES BEFORE HE DIED HE WAS STILL ALIVE' THE GUY RUSHED
    PAST ME ON HASTING SAYING

YES THANK YOU, NO PLEASE

Egg Foo Young Burgers at the Mutual

(LET'S PEEK UNDER THE PORNAIDS & SEE IF OUR IMAGINATIONS HAVE
    HEALED)

WHERE WERE YOU WHEN THE HOSTAGES QUIT?
I WAS DREAMING OF SMOKING A B-52

REAGAN, THE ACTOR
LINCOLN'S ASSASSIN COME HOME TO ROOST

WHO SHOT JL?
DALLAS?

WHAT DID YOU LEAVE TOWN FOR?
10 DAYS

SOME PEOPLE GO AROUND FUCKING THEMSELVES UP TO MATCH THE
    WORLD
SOME PEOPLE GO AROUND FUCKING UP THE WORLD TO MATCH
    THEMSELVES

WORLDS GO AROUND
PEOPLE COME AROUND

LET'S BE GONE TO BED AN HOUR EARLIER EACH WEEK & MAYBE WE'LL BE
    COME KIDS AGAIN

May We?

WAY DOWN AT THE DRIPPING END OF TOWN
SOMETIME SOMETHING
BEAUTIFUL BEGINS WITH YOU
SO BE THERE

RIDDLE: GIGGLE
ANSWER: LAUGHTER

PEA POLE
PEEP HOLE
PEOPLE

I'D WALK 5 MILES TO KITSILANO FOR A PISS IN A TOILET WITH A NATURAL
    WHOLE WOOD SEAT
LIKE THE BRAVE MICE TRAVEL FROM BATHTUB TO BATHTUB THROUGH THE
    DRAINPIPES LOOKING FOR A WAY OUT & LIVING OFF THE SPIDERS IN THE
    MEANTIME

WHEN YOU SAY I'M GOING TOO FAST I GROAN DOWN
WHEN I SAY YOU'RE GOING TOO SLOW YOU GROW UP

SNIFFIN' THRU THE STATIONARY DEP'T LOOKIN' FOR ALL THOSE FOLKS WHO
    LOVE POETRY

MAIS OUI!

HOOPS

hike

the way it
says it ...
not at all

   knilblink

   explain that crocodile is standing still to the kids
   share the flash
   no blink

the military-comedian complex

Johnny Carson calls it the year of
sitting here holding your cock
& the neutron martini: it gets you bombed but you don't fall down

polar bear exercise

tossing baby helicopters from the balcony to the seagulls on the wing
feed each seal from the first half of the herring bucket & then feed them
    all from the second half
you can't talk your mittens on so stay in the sunshine out of your
    shadow

big swings

hang on your cage by your beak & whistle
all in all we're having a great time called: the only thing I wanted to do
    was feed the squirrels peanuts but they're on strike
& as for me reading it out loud & clear to everyone on the bus home –
    whoops!

good idea

Peacock Crayons used to have a cold February hot-setting-sun-on-
    cedar Green
that's still there
on a clear day

       a week's word

       work on it
       play off it
       it's an old toy & it still goes

              eh

              ape busy seed he gift
              jesus age eye jade ache
              hello men hope peek use
              art rest eat chew feed
              dribble who egg wise head

YEARS

I want to make an honest reader out of you

I can't help it
I can get there & back in an hour on foot
but give me wheels & it takes all day
to ride it all down
to write down
what just seeing
what you would say
would say

      t-shirts

        if music be the food of love play on
        if play be the music of food love on
        if love be the play of music eat on
        if food be the love of play sing on

        if play be the love of food sing on
        if love be the food of music play on
        if food be the music of play love on
        if music be the play of love eat on

        if music be the play of food love on
        if play be the love of music eat on
        if love be the food of play sing on
        if food be the music of love play on

        if play be the music of love eat on
        if love be the play of food sing on
        if food be the love of music play on
        if music be the food of play love on

don't stumble over any stalled escalators

you've already said no
so I won't tell you what I was going to say

o these raining days
I was so hung-over last Sunday that watching the rain washed me
    away

wake with a splash & lie there
the whole book I've been reading finished last night like a dream

& just think of it
& lie there thinking of all the things I want & decide against them all

I'll take the cash instead
& spend it hiding Februaries in strawberries

kiss the cold
& catch the kid

I've been kept too dry in a plastic raincoat
I've never been to Williams Lake but I've been to William Blake

ghosts

the phone goes
the taps & drains go
the furnace goes
the electricity goes
the fridge goes
the radios go
one of the tv's goes
the record player comes & goes
the hot water heater goes
all the swingin' hinges & groovin' rollers on all the kinds of door go

the clocks go
the stove goes
the windows go
I go

having

    photography is wrong there
    things don't have their different colours

    things have their different speeds
    things have their different mice
    things have their different words
    things have their different fingers
    things have their different prices
    things have their different thoughts
    things have their different looks
    things have their different sounds
    things have their different people

    people don't have their different colours

    people have their different things
    people have their things differently

editorial

I left the window behind the curtain wide open last night
so the cold could get in to bed with me
& press me front & back into my skin where I belong

I got up early today & let the room sleep in for once
while the sun & I arranged a little surprise
& when everything is ready we open the curtains wide

& here am I sitting quietly in place

in the light
with everything else

& it's spring
with a ring to it that keeps on ringing
lifting the load off my face

bringing me together
keeping me apart

6 years later on

knowing where to be yesterday earns a week of drink & spends it all
    on one glass
all i hear in the music tonight is the motor it takes to turn the table
knowing where to look tomorrow earns an era of smoke & spends it all
    on one idea
one day's bath is better the next
knowing where to go today earns a life of work & spends it all on one
    another
but mostly i live in silence

valentine

there's a butterfly hiding in the top of the bush inside my head & he
rustles the thin green leaves like silk each time he sees all those bright
birds fly through your heart

WEEKS

tues

on a scale of 1.0 I'm .45 today
family I'm at your beck & (but) call (1st)
heroically it took 45 kisses to wake Sleeping Handsome up this
    morning

I vacuumed the place yesterday & swept it today
fixed the light in the toilet & polished my boots
installed a new pair of laces & gave my teeth a trip to the dentist

these crumbs on the page
dots of yin in all this yang
bits of the gods for food

the 1st birthday after the end of my 1st marriage I cried & cried
this is the 1st poem I've written with this typewriter
it's the last typewriter you'll ever need the salesman assured me

a poem begins like the 1st & ends like the last
one ever written

        wed

        ok
        you guys

        stand easy
        slow & easy

        Gustav
        Mahler

        wants to play
        gray

& green
with you

so let
down your cuffs

& grow up
the rain

thurs

tobacco
LOOK MA – NO LUNGS!
it's harder not smoking it the 2nd year
you can't scratch scratch

the itch is fear
the cure is courage

tobacco sucks you from the past
the lost future made visible as smoke
disappearing without a history

if the light you are reading this by is powered by nuclear fission
or by the death of some fish's river
close your eyes & say goodbye to poetry

fri

pick a Friday
any Friday

let the wind blow
away the fog

buy that lifejacket
wear it

repair your hair
set your watch

trim your lamps
perfect your curtains

have a banana
cancel a space shuttle

you are in
over your heart

     sat

this is a Native neighbourhood
this is an old neighbourhood
this is an artistic neighbourhood
this is an addicted neighbourhood
this is an Oriental neighbourhood
this is a working neighbourhood
this is a food-buying neighbourhood
this is a political neighbourhood
this is a religious neighbourhood
this is a mental neighbourhood
this is an indigent neighbourhood
this is a sirencrusted neighbourhood
this is the Downtown Eastside in motion
this is an only neighbourhood

sun

snow on the daisies
April Surprise!

a key in the lock
a breeze in the wind

if I can touch you
you can touch me

too much coffee's like
Bob Hope for president

this poem I'm writing
something to sit down with & to

or stand up to & with
in

is a park
with 100 ways you can take it & leave it

mon

that was the august time I carried my bike from the Spanish Banks
end of Wreck Beach, past all the Historical Landmarks, to the Players'
Club Cliff, & carried it up to the road & slipped through UBC like a photo-
copy, arriving at the Varsity Theatre, where I saw the movie of what you
were about to say before I interrupted; so this is the time I look up from
the page, my having carried my bike a few yards down Kits Beach to a
log somewhere between half an hour 'til sunset & an hour 'til low tide

look up & never look down again, except to fly with those birds, on a
loose schedule, cycling around the city delivering April

I think I'll just push East up False Creek & surprise the burning windows of Capitol Hill, with a tip of the cap I wear (to keep my head up) backwards (to keep my sky on) to the last roll of the sun, just before it carries today away

tu

so there I was, sleeping
dreaming of wonder drugs & weird diseases

& who comes in?
my absolute best friend, my brother

my imaginary brother
the one who's there to say, later that morning, just after I've had
    breakfast & clipped the news off the radio & had a bath & changed
    jeans & shaved

to say 'brush your teeth'
just loud enough so I can see myself not pause

just do it
that's the way to move

singing down the alley, routine landing
there are other discoveries, phone calls, decisions, bike rides,
    deliveries, $1.49 Days, movies, & (somewhere in there) dinner, to do,
    today

as well as possible/impossible as well as
writing not only this but also not only that

we

stoned again
cancel all ancient animosities

driven by my dreams
but why dream alone?

form a dream pool
marry an army

take a break from all this waking
working all night

writing all day
just trying to get unstuck

from the subject
the subject is love

love is the subject
act you a lie

I was spilling hot coffee on your finger
which was there brushing it away

wake up
with me

th

riding the spiral
the cochlea
the corner you never quite get around
until you've been turned from air into sound

faux dentures
surprised by pizza

we see each other straight ahead
can't fiddle with that

good friday

all that was left of the yesterday that's become a taste
was eaten by the sound that goes down forever
which also ate the alarm this morning
(losing count, next thing I'll lose my waist)
& ate the garbage truck & the buzzing fly
& ate me too except for a few fingers making this sign
& the ear in the sunshine

while I dream on
hard as a fist
my head on my hand on my wrist

fall asleep
climb awake

one place
all time

bad saturday

masking tape on the windows to keep the flies out
plastic on the roof to keep the rains out
mirrors on the walls to keep the room out
words on the page to keep the mind out
hot water on tap to keep the grease out
reggae on the radio to keep the heart out
cod on the stove to keep the wolf out

the furnace fan is noisy, it needs looking at
the blackjack is ready, it needs nothing more
the floor is dirty, it needs washing off

the Snail album cover is empty, it needs nothing but
the day is sunny, it needs working on
the poem is ok, it needs nothing much
'the', though, in line 5, is needless, it needs deleting

easter sunday

reading a review of Richard Brautigan's new book
reading a report on Italy's more than 600 tv stations
reading an interview with Tip O'Neill saying the Democrats must now
    suck up to the middle class
reading an update on tissue-specific antiserum cell-repair injections
    into the rich
reading a picture of the man who lives with a crow named Gonzo & 13
    other birds with names
reading a lament that Spike Milligan's 232 mimeo Goon Show
    annotated scripts (6000 pages) might get dispersed
reading a recipe for curing male impotence with rhiniceros urine
reading the pun 'H$_2$Eau' in a Perrier ad
reading a history of CND/UK & the new European disarmament
    movement END
reading a secret that physical work releases a morphine-like substance
    into the bloodstream
reading a Britannique reporter's prediction that the PQ will lose last
    week's general election
reading between the lies
reading a tune into what the churchbellringers were playing at 2
    o'clock this morning
reading a rumour that in Norfolk the Great Black Slug is fried & eaten
    on purpose

slow

how slow?
slow as Sinatra in '54
slow as 2 thin cigarettes rolled outa 1 fat 1
slow as the saboteur this poem slips into what you always thought

slow as the long deep look into space I took
through the instant my eyes vanished into that guy's
hunkered in his doorway as I glanced past
as he lifted the glazed donut to his lips as I walked by

slow as an improvisation no-one is noticing
slow as worse than losing

slow as the drunk with 3 things left to say –
'don't make any mistakes with me'
'always keep your feet on the ground'
& 'how are ya'

      better monday

        I didn't think of it
        but yeah
        I've thought of it

        it wouldn't work
        we'd misread it
        it'd come out all wrong

        all right
        I love you
        alright

        well
        maybe not all

you thought of it
think about it

it sure is a good idea

DAYS

at least

break a law a day
for 20 years
only get caught once

a boy in a tree playing me

fingerpit toepit
elbowpit kneepit
armpit legpit
fistpit facepit
spitpit stopit

someone's using a starting pistol
at the kindergarten track meet over there

if shit didn't stink
& stones didn't sink
& rock n roll had more soul

the children were here first

feeding nuts to the squirrels & fingers to the geese
gingersnaps to the photographers
& lovers to each other

the next afternoon

the sun shines on the park like poetry
the eraser's edge
whiting out what doesn't move

any excuse to live on the beach

8 ducks pass 6 ships & 12 boats =
'a bit windy' &
'only way to keep it clean'

oolichans

thanks
little fishes
you wuz delicious

& a rainy day

it almost never rains in Vancouver
even if almost never
seems like forever

summer of '81

when the school year finished
the sun came out
the kids are the only ones around here with any clout

what gravity

cat walks up the steps
like a river flowing down

the driver

feels us
inside
his bus

epitaph

plant
potatos
here

HELLO

well I walked home from the bus station
then Peter & I went right back out to see some old Buñuel films etc
now I'm in bed, me & the Queen's birthday

*

Thursday night
I never stopped dreaming
of us sleeping together

*

is your box of lemon-flavoured Vicks cough drops in the garbage bag
    under the bathroom sink empty or what
what if I've cured your cold
no wonder you know me

*

Friday night we discovered the window
I like silence
you like fresh air

*

I'm saving up for our first phonecall
it's time to take down the hanger I put over the bathtub to steam
    the wrinkles out of your blouse
in case we ever get dressed

*

sweet pillows
mine alone
Saturday night

*

I love our accent
taken softly it's an aphrodisiac
out loud it's the argument built into our laughter

*

Sunday
how dare I
love you

REALPOETIK

NO SUMMER

'NO SHIRT
'NO SHOES
'NO SERVICE'

COWBOY SONG

HIS HAT SIN STYLE
HIS HEAD SIN SHADE

HE DREAM SIN FACT
HE THINK SIN FICTION

HE TALK SIN THREATS
HE WALK SIN SWEATS

HIS HEART SIN HIS FACE
HIS PAST SIN DISGRACE

HIS FUTURE SIN SINCERE
HIS PRESENT SIN DEED

HIS MILK SIN HIS MONEY
HE'S MEAN!STEAD OF FUNNY

HE COME SIN LEVIS
HE LEAVE SIN DEEP SHIT

DOWNTOWN CORE

IT'S ONLY A THOUGHT BUT
THE WOMAN AT GRANVILLE & DUNSMUIR
NOON HOUR FRIDAY THE 13TH
CAN COLLECT HER PRIZE AS SOON AS SHE TELLS ME WHAT
I WAS THINKING
THAT MADE HER TURN AROUND & LOOK AT ME
LIKE I WAS ONLY A THOUGHT

ISES & NOTS

JAMES COBURN IS NOT LEE MARVIN
TONY CURTIS IS NOT BUGS BUNNY
VICTOR COLEMAN IS NOT JAMES JOYCE
GEORGE BOWERING IS NOT LI PO
ERNEST BORGNINE IS NOT ALLEN GINSBERG
RONALD REAGAN IS NOT STERLING HAYDEN
YOSEMITE SAM IS NOT ARTIE GOLD
JOHN BELUSHI IS NOT ERNIE KOVAKS
APRIL IS NOT SEPTEMBER
THE REST OF THE WORLD IS NOT THE REST OF THE WORLD
THIS IS NOT THE PIPE
A WILD TURKEY IS NOT A NANAIMO FOG
A NANAIMO FOG IS NOT GOING TO FLY AWAY

GRASS IS NOT GLASS
ISN'T IS NOT 'SNOT

PROPACANADA

LIMP
AS THE US FLAG
IN A TORONTO TV MOVIE

PUBLIC SURFACE ANNOUNCEMENTS

STRIKE
WHILE THE SUMMER IS HOT

IF YOU WANNA MAKE THE WORLD STOP
GET OUT THERE ON A BIKE & PUSH

SAVE
EL SALVADOR
ELSE

SOLIDARITY –
ONLY IN POLAND DOES A UNION SHOW MORE SENSE THAN A
    GOVERNMENT?
PITY

THERE'S FREEDOM OF SPEECH WHEN YOU
CAN DEFEND YOURSELF FROM WHOM YOU'RE TELLING IT TO

THE PENCIL IS IFFIER THAN THE GUN

MOBY POEM

DIDN'T THE POETRY SHOW YOU THE THEMES DREAMING YOU
DIDN'T THE POETRY FLOW THE ART OF SPEECH CREEK RIGHT PAST YOUR
    FRONT DORK
DIDN'T THE POETRY KNOW HOW TO STOP SPACE & WHEN TO START TIME
DIDN'T THE POETRY GO TO THE HEART OF THE VOICE IN THE EAR AT THE
    RAIL FROM THE LOOK TO THE SEA
DIDN'T THE POETRY THROW COMPLETE TO YOU ALONE IN THE END ZONE
DIDN'T THE POETRY SOW SEEDS OF SONG IN THE LONG FURROWS ON YOUR
    MIND
DIDN'T THE POETRY GROW OLDER DISGRACEFULLY REFUSING TO COME TO
    A CONCLUSION
DIDN'T THE POETRY ROW ROW ROW YOUR BOAT UNTIL YOU'D UNRAVELLED
    THE CLOUDS IN YOUR EYES
DIDN'T THE POETRY TOE THE LINE AFTER LINE OF CALCULATED AMBITION
    PASSING FOR PROFUNDITY IN CANLIT THOSE IF NOT THESE DAYS
DIDN'T THE POETRY SLOW DOWN LIGHT SO SOUND'D CATCH UP
DIDN'T THE POETRY BOWL YOU OVER WITH ADMIRATION FOR THE
    IMAGINATION IT TOOK TO GET TO THE BOOK
DIDN'T THE POETRY HO HO HO ITS WAY INTO THE WINTER OF YOUR DAY
DIDN'T THE POETRY POLARATE THE PUBLIC INTO THOSE WHO'VE HEARD &
    THOSE WHO'VE BLURRED
DIDN'T THE POETRY OWE YOU A SHOT AT EVERYTHING THAT'S NOT BEEN
    THOUGHT & A SAY IN WHAT GETS LEFT UNSAID

MAY WHAT I DON'T KNOW PROTECT ME FROM WHAT I DO

YELLOW INK IS CONTAGIOUS
THE BODY IS A DISEASE
PLOP

AINT NOBODY GONNA LAUGH FIRST

EVERYBODY PICKING ON EVERYBODY
TO WHOSE ADVANTAGE IS ALL THIS BAD NEWS
ALL OVER THE WORLD HERE
WHILE THE GANGS THAT THINK THEY'RE GETTING IN ON THE GROUND
    FLOOR OF CHAOS
THE GOVERNMENTS FAT WITH THE AUTHORITY THEY'VE EATEN
ARE PLAYING PSYCHOTICS VS IDIOTICS
ALL THE EVIL EMPIRES A RACIST TRICK
BASED ON THE FALLACY THAT SAYS LOGIC IS BASED ON LOGIC
TO BLUFF THE PEOPLES OF THE WORLD INTO DYING OF FRIGHT
TO MAKE THE UNIVERSE SAFE FOR THINKING ABOUT
AINT NOBODY GONNA LAUGH FIRST?

IF

HITCH HIKING IN VICTORIA IS HAVING FAITH THERE'LL BE A 90S
SO
HITCH HIKING IN VICTORIA IS LIKE ENDING THE ARMS RACE
BY
LETTING YOUR THUMB DO THE TALKING
TO
TELL WHAT ISN'T LISTENING IN US THAT IT'S TIME TO STOP
FOR
A CHAT
WITH
THE MAN TAKING A STAND

WHEN I'M HAPPY AGAIN I PROMISE NOT TO BLOW IT

THE NUCLEAR STAND OFF IS A BE BOP PUT ON
YANKEE WHITE COLLEGE BOYS CATCH IN BLACK & BLUE BARS
SO THEY WON'T BLOW UP THE WORLD ALL AT ONCE

MORAL

IF ON THE WAY TO
WARMTH WITHOUT WEIGHT YOU

SEE LOVE
SCREW IT

BOREDOM FROM WITHIN
(the week's top 17 enemies of poetry)

CAREEROOSTERS
COLLECTED TEACHERS
CYNICKLES
FORMALOOPS
FRIVOLISTS
HACKADEMICS
IRONAUTS
MYSTIFUCKERS
NARTS
PERISHING PUBLISHERS
PROFUSIONALS
PROPAGANDERS
SELECTED STUDENTS
SINCEREDIMES
SONG BUNGLERS
WEALTH WATCHERS
ZHOMBRES

QUANTUM POETICS

THE SPERM HAVEN'T SALMONED THEIR WAY UPSTREAM
UNTIL THE EGG IS DREAMED

THE POEM CAN'T START
UNTIL WE KNOW IT BY HEART

THE DAY ISN'T NIGHT
UNTIL EVERYONE GETS IT RIGHT

THE CHILD HASN'T GROWN UP
UNTIL THE FAMILY STOPS LOOKING DOWN

THE TOFU DOESN'T TAKE EFFECT
UNTIL THE BOOK GETS COOKED

THE BIRTHDAY IS ONLY HALF TRUE
UNTIL YOU GET THE OTHER HALF WHEN YOU'RE 92

THE EGG WON'T CRACK
UNTIL THE SPERM ATTACK

MILES TO METRIC

SAME SPEED
DIFFERENT BEAT

METRIC TO MILES

SAME BEAT
DIFFERENT SPEED

USA TO CANADA

SAME DIFFERENCE
BEATS SPEED

CANADA TO USA

SAME BEAST
DEFENDS SPEECH

A POEM

THERE IS A CARTOONIST IN THE CORNER IN THE JOINT HERE
SKETCHING SKETCHING

A BAND IN THE MIDDLE HERE
PLAYING PLAYING

A WAITRESS IN CHARGE HERE
TAKING OUR PRAYERS

& IN THE FINAL ANALYSIS A POET HERE (& NOT ME)
WHO AFTER EACH SOLO & ONLY AFTER EACH SOLO

STOPS WRITING HIS LONG TIME LINE AFTER LINE FILLING NAPKIN AFTER
   NAPKIN
LOOKS UP & CLAPS & CLAPS

BUT WHEN I'M ON DUTY
I DON'T EVEN PISS

BUT THAT'S THAT
& THIS IS THIS

PROOF OF PURCHASE

WILL THE PEACOCK GET THE LAST CRUMBS OUT OF THE BAGGIE
WILL ALL THE BAD NEWS ABOUT IT HELP ANYONE QUIT ANYTHING
WILL THE NUCLEAR DETERRENT WORK

ANDY KAUFMAN WILL SAY ANYTHING ON FRIDAYS

THE GUY AHEAD OF ME AT THE CHECK-OUT ASKED THE GIRL TO CHECK HIS
   BAG
THAT HE HADN'T STOLEN ANYTHING
& I SAID 'POOR BUT HONEST' & HE SAID
'WELL NEITHER ACTUALLY
'I CAN'T AFFORD TO BE POOR THESE DAYS
'& IT'S NOT SO MUCH BEING HONEST
'AS NOT BEING CAUGHT BEING DISHONEST'

REMEMBER THE STORM THAT HALLOWE'EN

SPLASHING THROUGH STANLEY PARK THE NEXT DAY
WITH ALL THE SAINTS THE ROCKS & THE RADIOS SINGING
& THE SUN COMING OUT FOR A LOOK
UNDER THE CLOUDS WITH US
AT U.S.S. FRYING PAN
A YANKEE GUMBOOT IN THE BAY
BLOCKING OUR VIEW TO THE FUTURE
OF LIFE AS WE KNOW IT
ENOUGH TO TAKE THE KIDS OUT TO SEE FOR OURSELVES
THIS SUNDAY AFTERNOON OF THE FLOATING TREES
THE CARPET OF DEBRIS UP AGAINST THE SEAWALL
THE URGE TO KICK MORE OFF THE EDGE
THE GULLS CROWS DUCKS GEESE HERONS

ALL LISTENING FROM THE WET WIND

THEY WEREN'T YOUR EYES
THEY WERE EYES

IT WASN'T MY POEM
IT WAS A POEM

SAY THE WORLD
SAVE SOMETHING

SAVE THE WORLD
SAY SOMETHING

HI

THIS IS GOD
I'M NOT IN RIGHT NOW
BUT IF YOU LEAVE YOUR GRUMBLES
YOU DEVIL YOU
I'LL GET RIGHT BACK
AS SOON AS I WANT
PLEASE WAIT FOR THE NEXT TIME YOU FALL ASLEEP

STARING UP A STORM

THE RAIN IS IN IT
FOR THE WIND
TO BLOW TODAY OUT

THE WIND HAS IT IN
FOR THE RAIN
TO WASH TONIGHT AWAY

INFIELD CHATTER

three times better
beats
twice as much

there is no last train
there is no history of real time

prepare to flash
when amber light stops

a fast walker
can survive a toronto

DO NOT ENTER BOX
UNLESS EXIT IS CLEAR

& on the lie with us live

& the drunks hog the booze

& the news is made of silly putty

*

the peak
blame your pain

I'm sorry sir
we're out of town

of your cap
on your habit

I'm sorry sir
your 8 hours are up

is to hide your eyes
break your habit

I'm sorry sir
your 90 years are not in yet

from the glare of the cameras
on your pain

*

the guy dozing in the smithrite
holy shit I was indignant

get outta there I said
he assured me it was all right he said

*it's all
right*

believe your friends
befriend your lovers

arms still wrapped in cellophane
are wings

the key stuck in the lock
like a 30 year record bad dream

if you can drink beer, chew gum & eat peanuts at the same time
you can quit smoking

4 FOR THE SKY

1. never sniff a stinging nettle with your own nose

the clouds rained milk
the phone woke in alarm
the fly died of the sleep in my eye

*

2. 'time is a glass of beer'

the rubber business-end of the swatter has a web design on it
with a spider in the middle thinking
'fly'll be right back'

*

3. another day changes into something comfortable to say

I left my tan in the Vancouver clothing store
by the rack after rack of thick stuffy jackets
made in Winnipet & Montorongrong
for the winter we on the coast even without luck
get for maybe one month out of forty
to the tune of NO CANADA while

the fly is faster than the vacuum cleaner
the spider is slower than the screen door

*

4. Mick Jogger

fly by night
spider by day

ARROW

everything gets done
doing things around the house all day
waiting for you

dial your number by heart
I know it's yours
you don't answer

they don't want love poems
that's why they never get everything done
someday they'll all live like me

autumn began early
I was swimming last week
Chief Dan George died this week

I know what I'll do if you don't come
I'll wait for you

*

take your time
here catch

a glimpse
reaching into bed

me ordinary
you plain

I make you & you make me
let me laugh & let you cry

where we kiss
names grow

sometimes I say yours
sometimes you say mine

I need everybody
I want you

*

touching
tames you
drives me wild
our voices shine right through us

*

by morning
out of meaning

through the ground
wishes rise

wide eyes
dawn on us

*

place me north of you
history is the lengths we go to
see larger & farther

your laugh shakes the whole world
rest in the west of me
take me smaller & closer

the porcelain white
behind a line
lighter & lighter than mine

*

'I love you
'I like you'
I said

you said
'don't hedge
'you scare me'

walk on
the water's fine

*

our legs were holding the stairs together

twice today when I rang
& I rang 100 rings today
I heard you pull the plug
I was glad you were home

what to do
get a haircut
finish this
stop that

meet me at
the vanishing point

APRIL IN CANADA

vancouver – calgary – regina – sudbury – toronto

but call

you mother

earth
earthy
earthly
earthling
earth link

i smell strong
you are

ear think

lirpaleef
lirpaloof

don't shine the floor when you can wash the sun

the coast was such a fraud
totally claustrophobic winter

8:40 in the morning on that midnight bus to april 1st 1982
soaking through to the continent

clear camel soup
revel steak
salmon army

chase stops the bus
the chase
the rest of the pencil

18 billion light years to calgary in nothing flat
mistsicles
ear pop

i remember when a tree was a tree
the trees are still the trees
trees will be trees

everyone can go everywhere & fight every war but no smoking
    in the first seven rows

the driver's getting old
the road is getting rolled
the story's getting told
getting is the shoulderpads built into the crewcut

hundreds of millions of people in the world
some right here
dying to defend shuswap community centre from us

we are the safety catch
we twitch & the world goes off
wet witch

i've seen the world looking for you
looking for you i've seen the world
looking for the world i've seen you
i've seen you looking for the world

for all the world to see
& seeing me
glance away
for all the world
as if you couldn't look

shuffle aside
deal yourself out
of a little old house
take your sombrero
& go sic a moose
to live in a trailer

save up for a truck

lucky we didn't sit together
i might have taken your tan
you might have caught me instead of this balloon
please, no strings

this can be said by saying so
all those cars on the highway are teachers rushing from student to
    student

the sem-eye did
slide in the ditch
on its side

we worked hard to get here
let's play back

it's always you
no matter who

your mountain standard poet s. flower
his name slides out from under him but he's
safe reliable courteous

a lot of the really important mountains were imported from alberta

meanwhile this week in calgary allow me to introduce you to the
    difference between
1. *win*
hookey is for kids
adam is 9 now
& only has to skate twice as much to get as far as there is
& the team is sure they're all nhl prospects
but there wasn't one penalty in the whole game
the kitten doesn't need to be taught to dance
& 2. *lose*
next month in vancouver
hockey is for keeps
the cat doesn't need to be told to kill

fuuuuuuuuuuuuuuuck

the aurora borealis at the glenbow is temporarily out of order

we start out identical
the first worb is a verd
ah shit
open the door
we finish indifferent
the last taste is a kiss
oh shit
the door's open

from dipping slippery toes in the st. lawrence
to dunking sneaky fingers in the bow

i get to calgary & i wanna grow
up there
i wanna be snowed in
i wanna be rained out
looka that guy!
writing on a piece of paper!
corner me & i'll gopher you
the grass
tossing the wind to the sky
just settle down
the tree says to the frisbee
the west
is where
the air
is from

at the party i introduce the engineer trying to re-capture the last bit of
    heat being lost from the building
to the athlete planning the building's energy-generating exercise room
all they didn't know was that they already knew each other

like to talk?
what are you reading?
this is sculpture
where are you going?
i'm coming from 20 years ago
overnight calgary-regina was here then

lovin' you
another year or 2

sometimes for a moment there isn't another light out there anywhere

we'd sit around the kitchen table making mistakes in our perceptions
    of the depths of our histories

i love travelling
i love being friendly

we were such good friends
swimming out of our bathing suits into our skins

once upon a time there were three potters
one wanted fame
one wanted fortune
one wanted fun
the pots they never made are everywhere

nothing has changed
this must be saskatchewan

i dream of you as young now that I can't see you as old

after the party i looked in the mirror & was amazed
i hadn't seen myself for hours & thought i'd got lost on the way
everyone so beautiful & me so what

i kept telling them they aren't crazy but they aren't mad
i'll send them my radio
it plays all sorts of stuff they haven't said

don't argue with the children
you'll wear out the language
sing to them
wear it in
yelling it is selling it
the kitten purred it & we all heard it

i found regina
where i left her

mother west
the little old city that do
whose kids have groo
into calgaroo
& edmontoo
& winnipoo

meanplace
meantime
father east
what am i doing in ontario?
what have you done with manitoba?

people all over the bus are making the night you know it's not just me
it's not just the hockey team that got all the extra seats we'd just
    curled up on
saying, 'well i suppose we could muster up a few if we have to'
when i told them this bus was for volunteers heading to the falkland
    islands
it's not just all that day he gets to take into the forest on the skidoo
    while i watch on by
but it is just the mother pulling the 2 year old on the sleigh with the 5
    year old hanging on to her fur & talking up to her something
    suddenly important as they step back along the trail drawn on the
    rolling surface of the snow beside & far above the highway into the
    distance the bus just came from

14:18
that's the time
sometimes

what thin telephone poles
barely strong enough for gossip

the aluminum can caves in like the barn i stepped on to stop our
    rolling around in the middle of the fright we all got the night the
    moon caught up with us
lighting each of our primateering faces

there, she's got a seat at the front of the bus & a seat at the back of the
    bus & she spends the other third of the time in the can
a page in a book is looking for her

she's always in the wrong place until she gets some sleep
i get to wake her when her ticket runs out

as for him, it's enough just to read hours into his ticket & make notes
    on an envelope addressed to the happiness nobody knows

the strap on my bag broke so i got a big double paper shopping bag to
    carry regina around in
i made myself at home in the cathedral district selling magazines each
    as heavy as the little tub of strawberried yogurt brought to you by
    the preservative party

smoke
my lucky starling

the girls don't realize what a sucker i am for a long conversation
but i have a boob a kook a book to end
just up ahead there around the next horizon
& back
to the guy combing his hair in winnipeg
'don't worry, you're beautiful' i said
that was a short conversation

the little old ladies right behind the driver are drawing the line
that the map is drawing us along

the kid in the can knows better than to whiz out the window what with
    the wind-chill factor low enough to freeze the family tree down to a
    teaspoon of instant flavour crystals

o god! i'm a canadian
see
i'm not arguing it, i'm doing it
watch
(laughter)
sifting through the dry-heavings of today's editorial pages that insist
    it's romantic to prefer disarmament to atomic war
watching the media hold toothpicks at arm's length & call them larger
    than telephone poles
agh! ye advertising propagoons! no-one reads you anymore except to
    find out what the censor has to say today
why don't you turn around & face the world & present our common
    sense

they wouldn't fire you all, you thought-traffic-controllers, would they?
anarchy is advertising telling the truth
politics protecting the minority from the majority
science dismantling hell
art defending the future from the present

the watch face's
zero zero/zero zero/zero zero
it's billie holiday's birthday

the guitarist is upset at 03:00 when we suggest it's too late for singing
'i'm not being paid' he mutters along
as the metal strings twang niceties
& we are spared the third attempt to recall more than one &
    three-quarter choruses of 'johnny's so long at the house of
    the rising sun'
then we all have a hot cuppa wawa
but when he sang
everyone could talk
& the bus sounded like a smoked restaurant in montreal
& we're almost drunk again & again
& we almost fuck again & again
& we almost want to see each other again & again
look down the aisle & you'll see the dream again & again
there i am, fifth row, south side, my own double seat since the top
    of the page
my head down in my vest pocket kept for future reference
not to be removed
boots hobbled under the seat
brushed & polished so you can see your fate in them
a few nights on the bus small torture as tortures go
my jacket leather between me & my knee

or is it the nanaimo ferry
or was it january

gum massage
feel good?
whales too you know

like

four and a half hours of sunshine in the past 2 weeks
japanese drumming in the park in the past 2 summers

the shatter of the tricycle
the piss of the traffic

poet's rattle
(unfinished)

cold water for a burn or a hard-boiled egg
candlelight for dinner tonight too

we eat
wheat

all right you –
i'll write you

up up &
earlier & earlier

in feathers
in silence

the ferry from
the moon to the sun

i won't be returning
i'm going all the way around

you can't swim back
we're in this leather together

eat
sleep

mind
doesn't mind
that it's one
in the shade

it's for me to say
'mind if i join you?'
'fine'

to
win

thee
the

in the
in the sun

two in the sun

january all along
february all alight
it felt pretty good when you tossed the door open & marched in
    shouting that you're even better
is that mars behind the moon?
the moon is made of a thunder we can't hear behind the light
like the guitarist keeps almost discovering the tune
lotsa pluck
yes kitty, that's a bird & this is an instinct
'that's enough' the singer says
& the white noise of the air conditioning swallows song
someone else
still you
someone else still
you too
when you win the title
the title is the plot
the ink rolls off the point like the gift of travel

if there's 3 things i can't abide it's

(1) burning my lips with a roach or
being an hour early for the half-price breakfast special
(2) security searching the bags under my eyes for booze on the night
    bus to prince rupert or
even one chromosome straying from the poem
(3) giving in to military-religious visions of armageddon with a flip of
    the 'everything's ok/sooner or later' coin or
you can't take a train in sault ste. marie to connect with the main line in
    sudbury anymore

it happened to you in reginagoo
you were saying your relationship with her was platonic & i thought
    you said botanic

you don't get that row of three snowmen on the front lawn without
    you get that big field of cars & parts & clotheslines & shacks behind
    the house

what are you missing looking down here

o moby jane is not your name

i'm 23 x 2, which adds up to ten & comes to one, like the year

i sorta half imagined that sudbury was half way down the hair of
    ontario
when of course it's right on the nose within sniffing distance of toronto
    on lake lip there

central canadian realism
a nice frosty well-sentimentalated climage that eats its young
like christians loving to be enemies

what language started the falkland war?
war? what war? the english language is always at war
now there isn't a border in the world you couldn't say something like
'any part of the usa you can see from canada once was canada' about
wasn't it the british going into suez that triggered the russians' tanks
    entering budapest?
like this year the brits are covering for the israeli's invasion of
    lebanon?
anyone who's been anywhere will tell you that in the third world
    when you drop your wallet in the market it's finders-keepers
which, being interpreted, means

the british government was willing to blow up the world to avoid
    joining in the general hilarity at its own carelessness & stupidity
while the argentine inquisition welcomed the promise of general
    slaughter to postpone its own reformation
the first casualty in war being the first thing that could have prevented
    it
a sense of humour
like if the prime minister & the general really mean it, they should take
    off their armour & fight it out in the bathtub with water pistols
which would still sell newspapers
& the britishcasting corporations could still show all their old english
    war movies

analysis –
the rapist can't get it up without violence
a familiar thing
like you can't get up in the morning without a cough & a coffee
or you can't get to work without a car up your ass
or you can't get to sleep without cutting yourself off
or the english royals can't fit the birth of their latest brat into history
    without conjuring up a bloody sacrificial bleeding
'2000 dead & dying?
'thanks awfully mummy'

laotse said –
'of all things, weapons are instruments of evil, hated by men ...
'soldiers are weapons of evil ...
'even in victory there is no beauty
'& whoever boasts of victory
'is one who delights in slaughter'
& 'a victory should be celebrated with the funeral rite'

of course that was 2500 years ago
before we needed a trident fleet
one sub will kill a continent
to protect us from ourselves
use only as directed

of course if south america really wants a fight
give it the british fleet
to help the native indian peoples to resist their aristocracies &
    militaries
& make the southern hemisphere really unsafe for a predatory
    northern hemisphere

the poor baby that dies
in venezuela
as elsewhere in latin america
is dressed, as best
with small wings
as angel, goes home
to heaven
the death causes
celebration
in the house
of the long lives that live after
behind
in venezuela

and they give
their body
the baby
to the poor house of the neighbours
for cause, for them
as well
to celebrate
something
in venezuela

tropic
decay is prevented
they boil the body
in water
my radio plays
venezuelan folk
music
i live
far away
living
from people
that live far away
in venezuela

but watch out for
wanting war
just because you don't care any more
the cat
taught me that
& speaking for the aces that thought of this era & gave it us
watch out for 1984
don't fall off the end of history
watching the death's head in the ontario provincial police logo
think the unthinkable

old couple, français, in the seat ahead
she fusses over him, straightens his collar, jams his toast, gives him his
    cushion
he floats in the attention, makes it there & back down the aisle with his
    cane, not a whisper of impatience, & a ready word in conversation,
    & a repertoire of impish gallic gesture meant to be seen face-on, as
    happily attentive as a dog with a bone
his wife appears to be the together one, but i notice that she doesn't
    talk to anyone, & when one of them has to sleep in a single seat, she
    gets the double seat

the calypso guitarist is singing again
'because you're mine i cross the line'
it's not as easy to tune in a guitar as it is to tune out a radio

big guys –
a man in those woods
bullrushes in that ditch

pancakes syrup bacon & am i ever thirsty 2 hours later
so i have a can of pepsi to chew on

slowly the day turns
into one of those ruined sheds
old skins
all along the trans canada

canada
if we don't got it
it ain't catching
if we ain't beneath it

it's not low
BOMB HERE

i blow quickly up
between each blow me down
burst of sleep
in my golden paddy cotton cap

drive-in retaining wall
made of blocks made of
wire bags of rocks called sudberries
like i fixed the endless strap on my vinyl tote with a paperclip

how i remember
you weren't there
i'll never forget

the cliff ice grows
gross forms of gravity

here's a tip
keep the change
i do

remain seated
& do not talk
to poet when
poem is in
motion

blue jays opener

home
in astro-greenola
the blues & the brews
good fly day

catch a falling ball
& put it in your poem &
never let it stop falling

$2 seats tossing calendar darts onto the field this afternoon
instead of snow

everybody's so important at a baseball game
it's as if we each arrived by parachute

singing *coo roo coo coo coo coo coo*
like the national anthem
the mckenzie bros. make the first throw up

b.j. the mascot
i heard he's a girl
raises the cheer
'we want beer!'

a hit on the second pitch & the crowd goes
'o no – not again this year!'
blue shining through empty seats

5 minutes into the game & the brewers are averaging a run a minute
but do the jays have?
18 pitchers

jays first at bats – not one called-strike
foul & ball & swing & ball & fly out
ball & ball & out at first
ball & ball & swing & single!
ball & out at first

i've never seen a batter give up

singing from the bleachers to the old pro –
'i remember the good ol' day you weren't a jay'

milwaukee is cincinnati without the sin if
cincinnati is milwaukee without the milk

& there's the united umpire loyalist fan club

3 guys in pure black slack sweater & cap
chanting 'please do not delay the poem by throwing prose onto the
    page'

everybody can have a bad day
anybody can have a good day

'run run run!'
whoops
lucky he didn't hear me

your mind on the gab
your boot on the bag
your eyes on the balls
your ass on the slab

some witt hit
the season's first homer just 10 rows below my banner saying
'lite up a j today'

there were people at the game i haven't even been before

we left half-way at seven/two
i mean
final score was fifteen/four

pretending what
good luck it was
it is
to lose the home opener

i get as lost as a shopping list & miss the boat back to the city

son of a gun!
i roll by on a monologue

visitor's rights of easement
you peek out from your life

have a thought in words
half a thought inwards

onwards
on ward's

phonography by og

– over here?
– hello?
– hi ... yes ... ah ... mm?
– a floating rep, eh?
– i can have ideas about whatever i have ideas about?
– i can turn everything into a question by raising my voice at the end of
    the line like dodging?
– birdshit?
– sure?
– who else is gonna do it?
– yeah ... right ... mm hm ... mm hm?
– she'd be great at that?
– yeah?
– that'd help me make up my mind if she'd do it?
– haha?
– yeah that's what i'm doing today too?
– i always put on shaving lotion first?
– you never know where he gets lines like?
– 'the north pole is a nice place to leave but i wouldn't want to
    arrive there'?
– well somebody has to have nothing to suffer about?
– water does what's happening to it?
– the beatles went through musak & came out lullaby?
– it's a kind of music in a style without cymbals
– well this is toronto & falling-down-drunks are issued hardhats?
– pick up some minced fridge on the way home?
– bye?

walking through cities

'a penny a kiss
a penny a fuck
we're gonna save our pennies in a big brown truck....'

partying is such sour sweetness

when you're stoned
you know you wouldn't a-got stoned
if'n it weren't already the stone age

i wonder who to bump into

everyone's taller than me
i was taller than everyone when i was the teen here
crossing eglinton one lane at a time
i didn't like it but i liked it

ah – there's a breath of air i had in saskatoon last week
this is for you in montreal tomorrow

i may never get back to gerrard street in time for 1957
when poems ended with lines like
'this april please do not criticize the wall paper'

        you see

        'what do you want?'
        the phone says

        'why do you want to see me?'
        it insists

        it's gone now
        play along with the song

'i just wanted to tell you a lot of money'
i would have said
but i needed what little there is to say
to eat off

i'm talking to myself
i already forget what made me cry

'we aren't friends to begin with
i don't know why i love you
i'm not you
you're not me
see you'

stop glaring at this writing
go read a painting

i love paint
the medium evaporates

you see you
see you see

            if you know what i mean

            no more dope
            no less booze

      never better (west queen street scene)

      watch me tell you the time
      nnnnnnnnnnnnnn
      ow!

      walk right by
      don't say hi
      see if i ...

me neither
i'm a jerk
you're a bore

maybe
you didn't even see me

ripple
rock

you didn't pause
you look great

i rushed after you
in the direction of your reflection

better
never

                    i always did

                sorry
                kid

bright black night egg

stop to write
zing-a-long cold
start toronto

canada is an aries

don't get much summer
don't need much

heavy boots
walk legs strong fast

ah, this morning i woke up with you making love to me

no i didn't
i'm not awake

i got to cabbagetown then i lost momentum somewhere

between the drunk & the tv faking they're talking to me
between the made-in-ontario BOMB HERE cruise missile guidance
    system & the canadian evolution
between the lie that anyone could survive a nuclear war & the truth
    that millions didn't survive the nuclear peace this year
between the arts nobody cares about & the cares nobody arts about
between the beautiful woman in white going wet beside me in the
    mars cafe out of the blue & what i was gonna do today
between the luck of the page & the business end of the language
between the sweat i'm bathed in all night & the nose stuffed in my
    mouth
between the damsels of avignon & tom dean's new paintings
between walking down spadina & not exaggerating
between the time it takes to read the globe & mail when someone's
    watching & when you're by yourself
between the 18" robert has grown since i last saw him & one price that
    hasn't gone up is that i want my voice to stop traffic on a dime

between learning from & doing to
between making up facts to prove your point & starting to curse again
   to spread it around more evenly
between tomorrow's friday & not yesterday's
between what you'll never know & what i can see through your hairdo
between being crammed into the phonebooth with everything except a
   quarter & only having a nickel's worth of anyway to say to outer
   canada today
between the train of thought & the unwitting station
between wrestling terror & wrist wrestling
between where you am & where i are
between we're all well past here now wearing our highschool perfect
   winning smiles & biting at the tears in ontario
between the way canadians hate spring & love fall
between walking along whistling anthropology & sitting alone in your
   walkman
between prose as sustained saying what you're thinking & verse as
   sustained thinking what you're saying

                        a world aloft

                        we fly together
                        species of a feather

                        give the weather the wing
                        & slip into spring

video drift

so ontario is east
i thought east was across from north

then the maritimes must be west
the west atlantic

the east pacific
the west of my life

let's watch that scene again
keep your eye on john candy pretending he just got laid off

        executive bonsai (a medium front street snicker)

        o wot a good job
        you can wear your jeans
        with a black gabardine suit jacket
        striped shirt
        tight tie
        & go where you're pointed
        & feel a little smaller every day

    yorkville

    if you're looking for a disease
    you can catch from yourself
    invest in money

make-up

you want it?
really?
you can have it

chip soup

older than toilet paper
younger than mathematics

a balance of air or
peeing is relieving

terror
whatever you say

around about it is
whatever you say

like
look at president raisin

that ass is the master
of faster & faster

his gods are numbers
he'll bomb heaven if necessary

shit eats
feel him grow there

eats shit
see him flow there

all together now
flush

like thermonuclear processes are alien to this plan plant planet
like monotony

if the arsenals are supposed to scare it out of us
how come those in charge of them are so full of it

      the world

        testing one two
        who else but you

        testing one two three
        mmmeee mmee me

        testing one two three four five
        is it us alive?

        testing one
        or is it the sun?

the middleclass dream still sleeps in toronto

everyone assumed
the college street car would stop at bay & it doesn't
so we take off our sunglasses & try again at yonge

everyone in t.o. wears all these ultra-warm clothes all winter
getting hotter & hotter
then on april 16th – flash! – & the city's in heat for summer

i better get outa here
i try to talk the church street busdriver into
driving to boston to see the baseball game we're listening to

2 fares left
outa the 90 counterfeit tickets
a guy tried to sell me for $5

may summer last
until all the frisbees have seized up
& all the hibaches have melted down

wax that zipper & ball that rock
but don't get too slippery or the stone won't roll
even tobacco smells good today

epithalamium

marriage is made in dreamtime
a cat's leap from catsleep
where rainfall reigns
& nipples rise like rice
& children are wild & wise
& promises are easy memories of the future
where you can see all the way around you

seeds grow time
slugs grow slime
poems grow rime
kids grow grime
dogs growl 'i'm'
husbands mime
wives sublime

a new city rising
from the lake

pull hard
life comes out like sun
love comes in like song

push soft
night comes on like light
day comes off like birth

one two
counting on you
three four
& many more

dreams time
dream times
dream time

the first dance

the fiddler never thought up what he played
who can remember what the poet said
the genius up there that everyone heard
was how they listened to each other out loud

the last dance

i don't know you
how come we knew what to do
lucky for us the music fell through

don't say anything
close the book
& look

stash your cap on the tail of the snake & you won't lose it

heading to the mainland
& the birds fly up as the boat bears down on them
they fly into the wind
& wheel in formation

& bank
& chug their way east
ink notes on the margin

farewells

you give
great grapefruit

as indians say about the cold
'it's good to feel the north'

8 hours sleep on a bus
comes at 20 minutes an hour

jet lag is arriving 2 days after you get there
bus lag is leaving 2 days after you go

it must be basically downhill from calgary to halifax
if you know the right roads

too cold for a winter festival this year
well that's what old photos are for

after running you don't feel like a smoke
you feel like a fire

it's possible to keep in touch
we know the words

bus depot

'can't always eat candy bars'
he said, buying a small tube of colgate's toothpaste
'i care what goes into me'

'can't always write up & down'
i said, hearing that in the house of lords you have to make your speech
    with your mouth not your eyes, so your words will feed rather than
    starve what you're talking about
'i care what comes out of me'

take a bus personally

drop it like a pill
fluff it up like a pillow
surround it like a pair of pants
wear it like thunder

'your place or mine' i said to the girl with the double seat

somewhere there's a pair of jeans to fit my ass like a romance
see-thru
feel-thru
sleep-thru
& with luck
live-thru
pant pant
not just another cup of coffee
not just another cup
not just an other
but really hot
really full
really fitting

well on the way

paper read
nails trimmed
face fed

boots off
laces loose
legs up

window eye open
head west
aisle eye shut

thin sun
2 kites
few words

your ipso fatcoat
algoma pillow
lake of snow

serpent river
high heels sinking into spring
local flow ontario

5 o'clock tantrum
el dorado nuclear
BOMB HERE

god i love you all
i can't stand it
i'll sit it out

c'mon
play forward
smile back

the church in the cemetary
the tongue surrounded by teeth
the world in people

a taste of nose
a breath of mouth
a glance of ear

wipe of window
scratch of arm
wreck of barn

thessalon
come & gone
but not forgotten

trees grove
snow grows low
prepare to meet thy creek

weather passing through
the windshield is the only glass on the bus that isn't tinted green
rednecks are hard work for a woman

here come the wiers
say your prayers
if you're a lamprey

bay
echo bay
echo

pastiche
presentable
futility

for reader safety
cosmic law prohibits operation of this poem
while anyone is standing forward of the white lie

root river brown
madnight blue
fear green

when you sue
ste marie
get some for me

wouldn't you know

lake superior
stuck in the snow

we almost caught the sunset
but at the last moment it lost us

lucky old bus driver gets to watch the road go bump in the night
while we squeak in our sleep back here

pressed between the pages of heavy metal
demanding rest at rest stops

dreaming that we'd finally de-fused the cold war
by everybody surrounding everybody else
& everybody surrendering to everybody else

i opened my eyes & i was awake
eagle hovering
over minnitaki in the morning

listening for falling word

the trans-canada highway is the movie of
the poem about the eternal amazement of
the dryden the moose at the trailer in the wobbling shape of

a boat that that van was hauling to
bee lake forest fire provincial park keeping to
the right except to

pass travelling west
by day where it was
by night going east

anticipating hiway 16 in northwest bc in june

somebody kneeling
in a roadside graveyard
& all this paper
on mine

don't sit beside me
i've got regrets
i'm always stopping for

the river roses
& overflowses
its bed of woeses

this guy up against it
& this other guy throwing something around him
& all he has to defend himself with is a baseball bat
but the bat is solid stone
i pulled it from the rust of the great steel skeena
i threw it back
i poured wine on it
i called it names
i stuck my gum to it
i sent it to a pile of medicine wheel to learn to rattle the world
because there isn't anything better to do

forest peel
burning in the field

are you sure you own petrocanada?

the kilometer kid
he goes around
shrinking the mountain
to fit the town

vandermobile
hoof home

never mine
never mind

getting there is finishing the book

manitoba

there is a centre of canada & we just pissed it
we all got out of the bus & wee-weed on the woo-wood
to see-seed just what way things are going here
& it is the centre of canada because the piss soaked straight in
but we kept going west to winnipeg
keeping our eyes open for patches of quickcity
traps where highly untreated canadians passed right through
     manitoba, sank & were never seen again
(how clever, they shoot golf on beige billiard courses)
anyway, first thing off the bus i shoot the crap i've been saving since i
     started living on donuts alone
then i lug what's left of me, holes & all, out into the sunlight
& start asking people where mcdermot avenue is & nobody knows
which is perfect because then i can find it for myself by wandering
     around aimlessly
& that done, have a denver san at ed's restaurant at the very foot of
     portage
then, against everyone's advice, i walk for half an hour
i could almost have walked across the assiniboine, it was so littered
     with statistics
but i had a malted milk in the bay instead
followed by a big stoneware jar of bernard's in the art gallery
& tender curried chicken & garlic sherry with jim & jane
& the dash back through my own way around what i don't know
like i know what those bikers without helmets don't know
which is what you never remember unless you're wearing a helmet
     when your heads hit
the road
jack

overnite to saskatoon

when all else succeeds
go to sleep
when all else fails
wake up

sunup sharp at 6

& the crazyman with his finders in his ears starts wailing at our
    shadow
    not to stop
'the faster you go/the faster it plays!'
feet tapping – boots splitting
& the busdriver hesitates but the crazyman can't hide in his eyelashes
    any longer
& can't let the bus slow down now
now that he's able to say it
'the faster you go/the faster it plays!'

the crazyman gets off quietly in saskatoon
(& don't we all)
down to raving his hands through & through his hair

the rest of us pile out & go inside the new depot
& just about pay it off with the cost of breakfast

'looks like it's gonna be a nice day today'
'we can stand a few'

it's not cream
it's an edible oil product
they're not jeans
they're an incredible denim sausage
leg-up, mother blonde
yes, you look like tina turner
i can't take my pen offa you

the besborough gives great phone book

the river looks the other way

the sign of the beast is sprayed on the saskatchewan gov't bldg
election coming up poem after all

even at the microwave-on-premises cafe (check your pacemaker with
    the bartender, suh) coffee is 50 cents each time
but i stray & pray
stay & pay
listening to a young couple murmering morning nothings to each
    other, shhhhhhhhhhhh
tinkling bands of gold
smoky lips
clear glasses
he tweed – she treed
facing each other in front of a big samoan chatter-pattern bark
    painking
    i mean painting
('arf' says jack spider)
& that's the way i see it
i don't have to ask them to get up & change tables to prove the view
it's the poet's job to say it right the first time

walking along the river
& a tiny creature in a tree scolds me for what i'm thinking

the think about saskatoon
is everybody sees me
they'd see you too
car peekers
cross walkers
shoulder rubbers

'hello'
they say
'held hi'
say i

i take off my hat to you
& we put on our shades
don't we

in the beginning is the void

i would have thought that an ndp premier would have scuttled a
    liberal ottawa ontario constitution, enshrining as it does the same
    old national muddle
along with saskatchewan's nuclear industry
so i shook allan blakeney's hand
so he lost the election next week
a hoser from the word buzz
but we never get to vote on whether or not to sell
like we always have
to every ali pedro & charlie
the dirtiest most dangerous nuke of all
your neighbourhood atomic power target
waiting with much more destruction than the earthquake that hits it

no can du!
BOMB HERE
who put the plutonium in pierre trudeau's pay envelope
BOMB HERE
cold lake cold
BOMB HERE
waiting for trident
BOMB HERE
mushrooms over comox
BOMB HERE
nuclear waste is death come to life
BOMB HERE
in the ending is the world

                         billions & billions served

                         the mountain ate mohammed
                         what you finally see is through

caesar ate christ
what you finally see is out

heaven ate buddha
what you finally see is in

hollywood ate marx
what you finally see is you

check content here

once you can catch a fly
you can catch a fly once
if you like flies canned
like cat is short for catch

it was 8 hours not 35 hours
she said they fucked for
that time they fucked for peace
on the kiss & telethon

would you recognize a toe if i drew it on the nicest day left this year?
like bugs whips out a paper & pencil & outdraws uncle sam, saying
'canada is the only country in the world people have time to stand
      around on escalators waiting for the drawer to close'
sculpture leads to poetry

or if you like for 'poetry' read 'the fuckin' bible'
so that line would say 'fucking leads to sculpture'

canadian poetry is such a print job

so i keep walking until sa-ska-toon & i decide to come back to each
      other in june to read this poem
even without hearing the news, people take off their clothes & lie in the
      sun

i get on the next bus to edmonton with dust on my boots & snow in the
   ditch
it's a back road to the alberta border
where the bumps turn into hills
& the gravel, as is well known, turns into gold or buffalos or $100 fines
   for littering the highway
the englishwoman & i share the front seat, taking turns dozing &
   growing with the afternoon
our conversation gives the driver a soundtrack with some great
   corners
like when i say, 'you may think the prairie is wide, but on a cloudy day
   you can see for yourself'
& 'it looks like it's gonna take longer for canadians to all become native
   than for edmonton to all become calgary'

            & 'gretzky defects'

            but not until after dinner
            & putting the paper to bed
            & going for italian coffee & ice cream & pinball
            & watching the canucks tilt l.a. off the ice
            & if a tonne is 1000 k, then it's little more than a ton
            & what's a tun?
            & edmonton?
            how does it hold a year?
            like a barrel of wine?
            let me tell you a story
            no, this is a poem

walking through cities

'it's getting pretty bad when you can't even buy yourself a cup of
   coffee
but if you walk around
you can found
always someone worse off than you'

his daughter-in-law's off on drugs again
& his son needed all his savings to hold the house
& there's no more need for catering companies because there's no
    more oil crews out
& he's scared to get sucked into the dole at 60
& he doesn't want to turn into a commissionaire yet
& the bum he's talking to in the mall is a kid of 16
deliver handbills tomorrow
or was that yesterday

author's note

i'll never get all those pictures i hung down or even right side up

one true move & you're in luck
one false love & you're a schmuck

sore foot, but that's just for walking
sore wrist, but that's just for talking

me & my book in my belt
samurai & ginger

cbc-fm is the tranquillizer of last resort in dazied canada

a bookstore doesn't mean it's written yet
a bridge doesn't mean the river's over
a university doesn't mean the universe makes sense

strong legs
strong words

ontario snow
manitoba clay
saskatchewan dust
alberta mud
british columbia water

'monsters are inoffensive'

Homing (lines written overnight on the toronto-montreal bus in 1965)

i talk

i stand on the sand looking at the cold water
the poem lies in itself
i watch my face on the window
i sit in the car looking at the road
the poem races the world

it is not quiet
it is not going to be quiet
'i do not want to be on this bus' – a kid
tell him i'm a big boy, not the man
& the wheels hum, it feels good, running
i've eaten too, have 2 seats to myself
& awake, canada, i'm 29
i'm the only one in the bus with the light on

get a haircut, my personal mother begged me, ok
okay, the game of boo i'm playing (remember)
with home, the dots on the lower lefthand corner
rupert, vancouver, my saltwater mind, the cold water, walking
beside, i floated over, i ate from, i glowed, sank in, dreamed i sank in
so cold the balls ache, i pissed in, coarse salt water
& see this road i watch (not the scenery) & water
(not the shag sinking coast, range of mountains my back was to, continent
not the sea) the place in, between, noplace
the inside passage, prince rupert/vancouver, between america & pacific
north, the way there
these passages, coasting along
the end of the west

'that man there played cards with your grandfather 40 years ago in rupert'
i am moved to remember the adventures of my ancestors
norman, english, celt, saxon
gilbert, capstick
'you have made your bed'

the father announced to the boy who ran away to sea from school, london,
    1860
he was master at 25, fleet owner, bluenose sailing clippers from nova scotia to
    the world
he retired at 35, lockeport, founding the bank
out of his mind came the boy, herman, who gets to south africa too late for the
    boer war
sails on to australia to trade at the goldfields
to marry catherine, my mother's mother
to invest his stake home in the maritimes shellfish industry & lose it on a year
    of the red tide
on to saskatchewan before 1910, battleford indian agent, merchant
children, away to prince rupert, 1920, the end of the wrong railway (road)
house rented not owned, same as my dad, as me
i am to be quiet when he comes home, grampa, not touch the jigsaw puzzle
turn off captain midnight, ckwx, our phone number was green 236
yes, he handed me a nickle at the suppertable, sunday, & fell over vomiting, i
    saw, & died
i waited upstairs at the window, 1941
his anglican potato patch
i bet we haven't had successful peasants in our family for 1000 years
the general strain
like: our word 'to shit' was 'to take a pain'

race the road there
under this bus
in canada

my father, leaving toronto, west, a dancer, gambler
when the others went to paris he sold magazines on the prairies in the 30s
photo: young man, young woman, sunshine, roadside
hitch-hiking british columbia, baby in the basket, suitcases, 1936
'no thank you' he said to the socreds who asked him to run in the first alberta
    general election they won
the lights pass through my dramatic face into my eyes
ghosts of the father who grew me everywhere
the road, i was across canada 5 times by the time i was 5

i'm no child
i'll be lucky to sleep at all
hours, whole nights, tonight, i hear the noise again
all words, tires, highway, water will not have changed

the people we are, if we could only stay

it was raining what can be said
the reflection in the window
the silver penshine
kingston/brockville

at 30,000 feet the whole strip of bacon is one road

prescott/macdonald-cartier freeway/1000 islands in the dark
the sparkling little lights of a bridge cross the black glass circles
*   i see from*
the fastest way to get west out of toronto is detour to montreal now
we'll never stop building the road 'til we're nowhere

the sun's going to come up in our eyes
only stop to yawn
it's a high dull ride
i will kill any bug which lands on my hand
i'm the only one in the bus with the light on
making all the noise

as the world learns

from the sea come the mountains
from the mountains come the trees
from the trees comes the wood
from the wood comes the lumber
from the lumber come the homes
from the homes come the poems
from the poems comes the paper
from the paper comes the flame
from the flame comes the fire
from the fire comes the sky
from the sky comes the sea

moby jane

1 pencil
2 poets

we learn to wait the occasional 30 years
the next line in mind a rumour

'sure can hear a lot of birds'
i said & they all shut up

afternoon in the grass past jericho
flesh held fast within our virginity

smelting for the silver running in the high tide at the foot of waterloo in the
*   dark*
where we leave ourselves

young & cold
long legs our asset in the sea

me & my net get a ride home in the '48 buick driven out from ontario to sell
*   before it falls apart*
hitting 100 on the dash up the quarter mile of alma road between 4th &
*   broadway*

goodbye to 1952
you go raise yourself a big family

i give away too many free samples
but i'm here when you call

& we're all eyes
& that's what we recognise

gazing through what we say
to what we've seen

friday april 23, 1982

animal awake
good morning

home in my own
time zone

that there's a horse's cock
this here's bc

kamloops

same breakfast i had coming through here 3 weeks ago
except then i had pacmancakes in the dining room & this time i sat in a
    corner of the cafeteria & caught the last of the sardines with a
    trusty toothpick

'did you get that tan in van?'
she sure did – it was 23˚ there yesterday
i shoulda turned off the pilot light

neat how in the can the other guy & i avoid taking adjoining cubicles
when you're a squatter
you gotta watch for flying water
i rush down to the river to see the turd off to the sea

hold that line

the doctor's there to give you a choice between dumb & stupid
he'd love my writing

visualize: *a   e   v   o   f*
close your eyes & reverse the letters
that's the part of the eye you read with

reading scientific american doesn't keep my bus from bouncing
   around
but it's better than wearing a wedding ring

let beauty take *its* course
you take yours
let beauty *take* its course
you take yours
let beauty take its course
you take yours

conversation is not what's drawing us home to our others
but it is piling all these trees between putting the fur in the freezer
   for the summer & climbing into a suitcase on stage to see if the
   audience ever rescues you

writing on both sides
from both ends
fills the ride
& empties the pen

picture windshield

jerry & jane was my grade 1 reader
save next week's tv listings from the morning paper

first they fire everybody
then they hire back those they want
like daylight savings go on tomorrow & off hallowe'en

jane
i always pulled over & let you pass
i'd never wave you into oncoming traffic

click goes the pen
the driver looks at it

heston was in a dream last night asking for a part in the book
he went to high school with warren in chicago

an intimidating place to play hockey
he can play peck
i was thinking of peck to play the white-haired lady beside me
with her spiderweb watchface & the pearly white dove diving down
    her lapel & a jotter parkered on her purse & such a tender arm to
    press
this sway & that

jane
this is really your story
i'm just here to shine my knee through these old jeans' last rip

will that be charge or?
cache creek
'you won't be here long'

would passengers please refrain from popping their ears with their
    eyes open

i wonder if the witnesses get together & have a laugh at what they've
    seen & stood all day
'i wouldn't mind her job' says the new driver
she looks away from jehovah & waves the bus a blessing as we depart
    for hope

watch that stream fight its way downtrain
follow that rolls
uncle fred built a spences bridge once too
so it is the same water
pass that royce

we say
'have a nice day'
we mean
we never meet again

write defensively
don't tell lilacs
pussy willow won't she
be prepared to bite your tongue

will the real mountains please stand
you can keep your caps on

the thompson took the fraser to lunch at lytton & never came back

poetry says
only innocence shall
smell essential

stone bouncing down the road
yesterday i kicked a big applejuice can around the alberta legislature

'canadian necrobatic team' (fraser canyon graffiti)

engineers
cruel
the world

we stop for 10 minutes at a destruction site
close your eyes in the sunlight
close pink visions of nipples fly at us

jane
the world may not always be on your side
but it's at your side

it's a ride
it's a road
it's a great canadian painting

fly high
fall tall

driver to boston bar passenger: 'where's the crews today?'
'jeez, they've taken the train, they're desperate'
form single friday

no stomachs turning in tunnels under any sluglances please

chickens pecking along the road to spuzzum
looking for a reason to cross